HOW TO
WRITE
BOOKS
THAT
SELL

HOW TO WRITE BOOKS THAT SELL

L. PERRY WILBUR

Contemporary Books, Inc.
Chicago

Library of Congress Cataloging in Publication Data

Wilbur, L. Perry
    How to write books that sell: a guide to cashing
in on the booming book business.

    Includes index.
    1. Authorship.   2. Book industries and trade.
I. Title.
PN147.W48   1979   808'.025   79-50999
ISBN 0-8092-7348-9
ISBN 0-8092-7347-0 pbk.

Published by Contemporary Books, Inc.
180 North Michigan Avenue, Chicago, Illinois 60601
Manufactured in the United States of America
Library of Congress Catalog Card Number: 79-50999
International Standard Book Number: 0-8092-7348-9 (cloth)
                                    0-8092-7347-0 (paper)

Published simultaneously in Canada by
Beaverbooks
953 Dillingham Road
Pickering, Ontario L1W 1Z7
Canada

IN MEMORY OF MY GRANDMOTHER,
who loved books and always encouraged me
in all areas of my writing.

Contents

CHAPTER ONE

Best Sellers Never Die and Rarely Fade Away

You've heard the old saying that inside every person there's at least one good book. Practically every day, in the halls of commerce, or almost any place where people live and work together, someone utters the familiar line: "I could write a book about it." Have you ever thought of doing just that?

Most never do. Many like to think or talk about writing a book and even say they're going to do it when they can find the time. But the time never comes.

In your hands now is a book that will prove to you that you can finish a manuscript of your own. And it follows logically that if you can write a book, you may also write a best seller sooner or later. The first book you write could be a dud, a fair-to-strong seller, or a blockbuster. You'll never know till you try.

The mere fact that you haven't written before could mean that you would bring a degree of freshness to the subject of your book. If you've already tried your hand at short stories, a play, feature writing, verse, or even the beginning of a novel, so much the better. All writing experience you've had just means you're that much closer to a best seller.

The Challenge of Writing a Best Seller

You may be concerned about the odds against your writing a best seller or even completing a book. Don't let it bother you. If Columbus had worried too much about the odds against him, he might never have found the New World.

Think of the tremendous odds against the brave forty-niners ever reaching California. They faced disease, storms, Indian attacks, accidents, and much more. Yet they were undaunted. They left their homes in search of a dream, the dream of a fortune in gold waiting for them in California.

If you have an adventurous spirit, this book is for you. Writing a book is a marvelous adventure. It's like having a child of your own and watching that child grow. If the idea of bringing something new into the world appeals to you, you'll gain real satisfaction from writing a book. There are of course many other books written on subjects similar to what you may write. But none of them will be quite like the book you write. Why is this so? Because there's no one else quite like you in the world.

Writing a new book is a challenge, whether it becomes a best seller or not. Just finishing a manuscript will give you a sense of achievement. There's nothing like it.

Consider this. Best-selling author Harold Robbins usually has no idea of what his books are going to be about when he begins on page one. The first page of a new book is always a challenge to him. He simply writes the first sentence and takes off from there.

The Prestige and Money of a Best Seller

The money and prestige of a big seller is certainly worth shooting for. About nineteen years ago, writer Mort Weisinger got a smash idea for a new paperback book. Mort had worked his way through college forty years ago writing science fiction thrillers for one-half cent a word. So he did know some editors in the publishing industry and got in touch with some about his new paperback idea.

His idea was for a book that would tell the reader about all the free things available for the asking from private industry, public relations firms, the government, and other sources. Some of these free items were games, stamps, records, various kits, coloring books, and travel information.

The editor of a major publishing company in New York liked the sound of Mort's idea and asked him for the title. Mort replied that it was *1,001 Valuable Things You Can Get Free*. The editor called a quick meeting of his staff and had a book contract for Weisinger within forty-eight hours.

The rest is publishing history. To date, there have been forty-one printings of the book and ten editions. More than 3,500,000 copies have been sold, earning Weisinger over $400,000. The book is still selling today. You may have it yourself or have read it. There's no reason why it won't continue to sell for another twenty years or longer.

John Dean, former White House aide and key figure in the Watergate scandal, has a new book out called *Blind Ambition*. At this writing, the book has already sold 130,000 copies. This means that Dean has already earned a tidy bundle from the hardcover book. It will almost certainly be out in a paperback edition in a year or less, so Dean stands to make even more money.

You might think that the public would be tired by now of hearing and reading about the Watergate mess. The initial sales of Dean's book proved otherwise. Who knows how many more hardcover books and paperbacks will be published in the coming years on the same subject? Washington seeress Jeane Dixon has reportedly predicted another future government scandal within the next ten years, so books dealing in some way with government scandal will probably be popular for the rest of the century.

Other long-time best sellers include *Death of a President, How to Win Friends and Influence People, Jaws, The Rich and Super-Rich, The Joy of Cooking, The Sensuous Woman, Gone With the Wind,* and many more. Many of these big selling books will still be selling in the closing decade of this fast-fading century.

What Makes a Book Keep Selling?

Look over any list of best sellers, and you'll notice that the books have strong attraction for millions of readers, for example, *The Joy of Cooking.* There must be millions of people interested in the art of cooking, judging from the huge sales figures chalked up by that book. And a book on cooking is timeless. It can be of equal value years from now. There are more marriages every year, and newlyweds will undoubtedly continue to buy the book every year. It's a continuing gold mine. The book's future sales are virtually certain.

Look at Your Future as a Book Writer

Let's say that you manage to write and sell at least one new book each year for the next five years. As an example, assume that four of your five published books sell just fairly well. One of the five sells 100,000 copies. Depending upon whether your books are hardcover or paperbacks (you may have some of each), you could easily earn $100,000 to $150,000 from all five. This is of course an estimate. If several of the books continued to sell in the coming years, you could make even more. You might not do this well, however. Nobody really knows what any one book will earn for sure, until after it's published and some indication of sales are on the books. This is another reason the publishing business is so interesting. There are frequent surprises.

The point of the above example is to show you that you would certainly have a wonderful future as a book writer. Once you develop your interest and ability to write books, you might be able to finish two good books a year. It depends on you and the amount of work involved in each book you do. Some writers spend three years or longer on a single book. But these are often long books. If you write your books on a part-time basis, (mornings, evenings, and on weekends) it will also take longer than it does for a full-time writer to finish one or more new ones.

Book Royalties Add Up

Erle Stanley Gardner, the creator of the Perry Mason books, usually had seven or eight new book projects underway at all times. He naturally had a staff of secretaries and typists to help him maintain this kind of proliferation. Jules Verne *(From the Earth to the Moon)* never hesitated to stop work on one book, if he got a strong idea for another one.

Proof There Is a Book in You

Why am I so sure there's a book in you waiting to be written? Because I know there are one or more subjects that probably interest you a great deal. You may even be an authority on some subject. If so, it's a natural for a book.

If you've worked and lived long enough, you're bound

to have accumulated ideas, wisdom, and opinions on anything from the art of living (how to live better) to farming. Many readers would therefore profit from a book by you on topics you know well.

You may know a lot about a certain type of business, the health field, or any one of a hundred other topics. Your own knowledge and information, along with the research you will do on the subject, could result in a helpful and interesting book.

Preview of the Pages to Follow

You'll learn in this book whether you should write a nonfiction book, a novel, or both. Chapter Four will show you that ideas for new books are floating around every day. Just one big idea can get you started. You'll discover how to get power into your book chapters and keep the reader with you all the way through to the last page of your book.

Above all, you'll learn what goes into a best seller and how to do everything possible to make your book arrive on that coveted honor roll, the best-seller list.

Chapter Ten will show you the modern way to sell your book to a publisher. This chapter alone can do a great deal to launch your career as a money-making book writer. Writing a book is only half of your challenge as a writer. You want to sell your book and see it in print, so it will have a chance on the national market. This chapter tells you everything to do.

Writing Books Is Still a Good Way to Make Money

Judging by all the books you see in the stores, the future of book publishing looks good. A lot of new books get published every year. While it's true that only a small percentage of them will become best sellers, there's always the chance that one of them will be yours.

Writing a book is as good a way as any to earn extra money today, and maybe even a bonanza. It's a fairer and more interesting pursuit than most. The majority of those who write books and other material are happy people who wouldn't change their life-styles for anything. George Sand, the French novelist who chalked up a number of best sellers in her day, said it well: "Books, ideas, and music; that's what life is all about."

Decide now to become a writer of books, even if you can only devote a few hours a day to it. That's enough to get many books written and published over a period of months and years. And who knows? One or more of them might turn into best sellers. It could happen. This book will certainly increase the chances of it happening for you.

CHAPTER TWO

The Truth about Writing a Best Seller

I now want you to banish from your mind the idea that one must be a genius to write a best seller. It just isn't true.

The following realities should encourage you. Get them clear in your mind:

- A best seller can be written on the first try. Peter Benchley did it with *Jaws* and will earn well over ten million dollars for it. He'll get another fortune when the television rights are sold.

- Not many really good books are published each year.

- Publishers are definitely looking for authors (new and experienced ones) to write the best sellers of tomorrow. You could be one of them.

- A best seller can cover any one of a variety of subjects.

- Many best sellers have been written by authors forty years old or more. But best sellers are also written by authors in their early twenties up through the golden years.

- Many best sellers are written in the home or apartment of the author.
- Imaginative publicity and promotion are what often turn a book into a best seller.

Writing a Best Seller on the First Try

The odds are naturally against your duplicating the success of a *Jaws, Godfather,* or *Thorn Birds,* but let's be clear about it. It can be done. Just don't count on it.

The late Jacqueline Susann turned out at least a mini best seller on her first try. The book about her dog was *Every Night, Josephine.* It was a worthy first effort and hinted at better things to come.

The important thing was that Jackie kept writing, in between her acting and modeling assignments. She decided that she knew the world of television, movies, and Madison Avenue advertising well, certainly far better than most. She had a clear knowledge of how the people of these worlds lived and what their lives behind the scenes were really like.

One day Jackie sat down and started a book that was destined to make publishing history—*Valley of the Dolls.* By the spring of 1969, her book had sold about ten million copies in paperback. The paperback reprint rights were sold to Bantam for $125,000. Sales have now passed twenty-five million.

Jackie worked hard on her books. She believed that best sellers require more than a few months of work. She spent two years on *Valley of the Dolls* and more years turning out *The Love Machine, Once Is Not Enough,* and *Dolores.*

So look at it this way. You have the chance to produce a best seller on your very first try. If you fall short of your goal, you may well have at least a mini best seller. If not, then your first book—however many copies it sells—can pave the way for a best seller on your second or third try.

A Shortage of Really Good Books

To prove to yourself how few good books there are, drop in to your local bookstore. Several facts will become clear to you:

1. Many books that are poorly done get published each year. And a lot of them sell well.

2. There are many book publishers—over 1100 in America (at this writing) and hundreds more in Britain, Europe, Canada, Australia, and other countries.

3. A great many new books are published every year—close to 40,000 if you count all types of books. And the number of books published seems to be growing.

One reason for the astronomical prices certain books bring in is their uniqueness when compared to most others. This is why leading paperback companies are willing to bid huge amounts to get these superior novels and nonfiction books. Paperback companies need a big seller every month, so they don't mind the risk.

Publishers Are Looking for Authors

Despite the already crowded shelves in most bookstores, publishers continue to turn out many new books each fall and spring. Some executives in the publishing business believe there are far too many produced each year.

But there's no doubt that the public is buying books like never before. The crowds in most bookstores prove it. While many are just looking, a surprising number of books are being sold.

Mass market paperback sales alone jumped from 495 million to 531 million last year. The 1980s will no doubt see a continuous rise in all retail book sales.

Book clubs are reportedly doing a brisk business. Sales of professional books were up by 12 percent last year. And the combined total sales of mail order business plus book clubs is currently over $750 million.

All indications and the views of experts point to a

continuing boom for the book business, at least through the rest of the century.

So an inescapable question is this. Where are the new books needed for the coming years going to come from? Hopefully from many new authors, as well as the present number of veterans. But many new authors will have to see print if the growing demand for more books is to be met.

A few startling figures should convince you that books are going to be in ever greater demand in the next twenty years. Population authorities report the following expected increases in the coming years:

In 1985: a population of 248 million in the United States, an increase of 46 million from 1970.

In 2000: a whopping 287 million people.

The above figures are for the United States alone. But population figures in most overseas countries will also reach new heights. By the 1990s, the earth's population will have almost doubled to a staggering 5.3 billion. By 2000, it will be six billion or more.

So it's obvious that a great many more books will be needed, to meet the international reading public's demand. This alone is a very strong reason for you to get busy now writing books.

Once you've gotten your first book credit, you'll also find a warmer reception in publishing company offices. Editors and publishers will be even more interested in signing you up to write a manuscript.

Editors and publishers are always looking for budding authors. They actively scan all sorts of publications for possible authors. Older authors die or grow less productive. So there must be a continuous source of newcomers ready to take their places and keep the presses running.

Subjects for Best Sellers

Best-selling books have been written on a variety of

subjects including (just to name a few) cooking, sex, all kinds of physical fitness topics, the pursuit of happiness, money-making, crafts, godfathers, family sagas, and many others.

One good example of a best seller is a book published by Grosset and Dunlap called *Jogging*. In only four months, the book sold 275,000 copies. The fact that jogging has been a hot subject in recent years added extra appeal to the book.

Other books that were best sellers include *The Gospel According to Peanuts* for John Knox Press and a Cornerstone Library book called *From Here to Happiness* (over 60,000 paperback sales in a few months).

Picking the right subject can give your book a stronger chance to become a best seller. You can learn to be clever at choosing subjects for your books.

Best Sellers Are Written at All Ages

Whatever your age may be, don't let the lack of enough candles—or too many of them—on your birthday cake keep you from producing a successful book.

At age eighty-nine, P. G. Wodehouse was still producing material. A novel he completed in 1970 was *No Nudes Is Good Nudes*.

What happens in many cases is that authors get hooked on writing books. It gets in their blood, keeps them young, and has probably meant extra years of life for many who took up the pen or typewriter long ago.

Sometimes an author doesn't find his voice—or even start to write—until forty or more. The late Bruce Catton didn't start his first novel until his forty-ninth birthday. He eventually finished *Mr. Lincoln's Army* and later turned out the Pulitzer Prize winning book, *A Stillness at Appomattox*. Between 1948 and 1976, he published seventeen books.

Bruce Catton proved that a person can turn to writing at a fairly late age and become a productive and highly successful author.

In the United States, the average age at which a novelist is first published is forty, and his or her novel is the third written. *Books in Canada* magazine recently published an article about a creative writing professor, who has written forty novels, with only one published to date.

Rod Serling started writing fairly young, while still in military service. Known mainly as a television writer, he came in time to prefer books over writing for the tube.

There are of course many younger authors around, along with the older ones. Stephen King made a name for himself with *Carrie* and *Salem's Lot*. He has a great future ahead.

Robert Benchley, the famed author and beloved humorist, once commented on the time needed to develop writing ability: "It took me fifteen years to discover I had no talent for writing, but I couldn't give it up because by that time I was too famous."

Where Best Sellers Are Written

Many newcomers who write believe they need a resort-like atmosphere in which to write their books. The truth is that a best seller can be written just about anywhere. Dr. Norman Vincent Peale has written a number of his successful books in a farm house in the country.

In time, most authors discover where they can turn out their best work, whether it's at home, in a rented office, at the seashore, in a cabin in the woods, or locked up in a big city hotel room.

Some authors are able to write anywhere and everywhere. Others have to stick to one or a few basic locations. Until you learn where the words flow best for you, you should experiment with different places.

Most of the research for the successful book, *Nicholas and Alexandra,* was done in the New York Public Library and at Columbia University. Yet many readers of the book were no doubt convinced that the author spent some time in Russia.

One author wrote the first five chapters of *The Case for Israel* in three weeks. He then went to Israel to look up places and to note any number of changes. The book was completed in four months.

Imaginative Publicity and Promotion Make Best Sellers

One of the clearest realities to emerge in today's book publishing business is the fact that authors with charisma and media appeal can turn their books into blockbusters.

One guest spot on the "Today Show" or "Donahue" can send the sales of a book soaring to new records.

Dr. Wayne Dyer, best-selling author of *Your Erroneous Zones* and *Pulling Your Own Strings,* drives across the country when he has a new book out. He personally visits bookstores and is interviewed on local radio and television programs. Dyer has now become a frequent guest on the "Today," "Tonight," and "Tomorrow" programs. The combined effect of this local and national exposure has helped to make him one of the most successful authors of today. He believes in his books and promotes them in every way possible.

What this means for any and all authors—new and experienced alike—is simply that learning how to be an amiable guest on local or national programs is well worth the effort. Some authors seem to click easily and with little effort. Others need more media grooming.

A lot of authors want to forget their books, once they've been published and are in the stores. They're ready to turn to a new project. Yet this is when the author should be doing everything possible to promote the new book, with the cooperation of his or her publisher. In fact, the best publicity and promotion campaigns begin long before publication date.

It stands to reason that your chances of getting a best seller are much better, if you can develop a media personality. While it's true that most authors can't start out with a guest spot on the Carson show, you can begin on local shows. If at all possible, you can load your car with copies of your new book and take off on a cross-country trip promoting your book at bookstores, on local talk shows, and everywhere possible.

With enough local exposure, in a number of key areas, your book sales should start to climb. And increased sales, if steady, can mean more willingness and enthusiasm on the part of your publisher to arrange for more significant media appearances.

With some luck going for you, and especially if you are a hit on the programs you appear on, you could find your book sales skyrocketing and a valuable booking lined up for "Today," "Donahue," "Tonight," the "Tomorrow Show," or one of the other top-rated programs.

Name value is worth plenty to an author. It's like money in the bank. It means book buyers will remember you—from the programs they've seen or heard you on— and they'll ask for your book in the stores. By that time, however, your book (or books) will probably be on a special display rack in many major bookstores.

The point to remember is that major media appearances and bookings can put your book (which may have been selling only fair to middling) in the best-seller league fast.

Some publishers back their books with major promotional campaigns. Avon, for example, put $350,000 behind *The Thorn Birds* and was willing to do it, in order to get back the $1.9 million already invested in the paperback.

Here are some additional truths about writing and building a best seller:

• Anyone who can write a simple sentence can produce a best seller. The potential is always there at least. After all, any and every best seller you can name was written by adding one sentence after another. Most authors like or soon develop an affectionate feeling for sentences as well as words.

● Word-of-mouth advertising has also helped turn a book into a best seller in numerous cases. People buy the book and tell their friends, associates, neighbors, and relatives or acquaintances overseas about it. The word spreads and sales keep climbing. The result is often a best seller.

● Views differ on how many sales constitute a best seller. Generally speaking, most consider a book that sells 40,000 or more copies a best seller.

● If you're an expert or recognized authority on a particular subject, your chances of getting a good book contract from a major publisher will be all the better. Such credentials always help, but they aren't a must. An author would quickly run out of subjects to write about, if he or she had to be an expert on each one. Many authors become authorities on a subject in the process of researching and writing a book anyway. If your project is a novel, you certainly don't have to be an expert on a given subject to write it.

● Many authors who don't produce a best seller still earn a lot of money in publishing. It's nice to aim high, but remember that many less lucrative books still make money and can sell for years. A mystery author once remarked that she didn't earn a jackpot from any one book. But the combined total of her twenty-five mysteries added up to a lot of the green stuff. Best-selling author James Michener says it this way: "Lacking short stories to sell, the next best thing is having ten to fifteen book titles in print. There's always the possibility that something will happen. Someone in Holland will pick up one of them for a quick $615."

● Whenever you read, hear about, or pick up a best seller in the stores, think about the idea behind it. Why is it so popular? Is it a timely subject? Does the author enjoy name recognition? How does it deliver its front cover promise? Break down the reasons for its success. Then try to get these factors into your own books.

● Faith in yourself and your book is very important. Without faith in yourself, nothing else really matters. Faith will sustain you, if your book should be rejected by one or more publishers. There are plenty of companies you can try. If one or more turn you down, keep sending your manuscript to other publishers. Always remember, "There's no such thing as failure. What seems like failure is merely one door being slammed in a corridor which leads to success."

● You never know what may catch an editor's fancy. So hang in there and keep trying.

● Keep in mind that publishers and editors make mistakes. The following top selling books were rejected any number of times. *Auntie Mame* was rejected by fifteen publishers. *The Day of the Jackal* was turned down by four major companies. Seventeen publishers said no to *Lust for Life*.

● Craft and hobby books have been selling very well in recent years. This category is one many new authors break into each year.

● A rejection letter is only one person's idea or reaction. Keep sending out feelers on every book project you believe can make it.

● Books that help people in any number of ways often become best sellers.

● There's still more prestige for the author in hardcover books. But remember. Paperbacks have revolutionized the publishing business and are the greatest entertainment buy in many countries. When you get ideas for new book projects, decide whether they're hardcover titles or more suitable as paperbacks.

● It's possible to get a best seller without an agent.

Some reports claim that 90 percent of all trade books were submitted to publishers by agents. Many authors, however, do very well representing themselves. The wrong agent can hurt a new author. The time to decide about an agent is after you've attained some initial success. Most agents won't consider you until that point anyway.

● The public's fancy can change quickly. You have just as good a chance to spot a trend developing as anyone else. In fact, newcomers often hit at just the right time with refreshing new books.

● By writing a book a year, for a number of years, you'll naturally increase your chances for a best seller.

CHAPTER THREE

What It Takes to Write a Novel

Each time you write a book, you have a choice of doing either a novel or a nonfiction book. Let's take a look first at the possibilities of writing a novel. Actually, your decision to write either type of book is an important one.

Some authors write mostly novels, while others tend to stick with nonfiction books. A strong clue as to which type of book you should do lies in your own reading habits. Do you read more novels than nonfiction or vice versa? The kind of book you read most often is probably the type you can do best.

There are of course any number of authors who can handle both types of writing. They've discovered through experience that they feel at home working on either a novel or a nonfiction book. These fortunate authors may write several novels in a row, a number of nonfiction titles in succession, or alternate back and forth.

If you like to read novels best, then you would probably

prefer writing this kind of book. There's no cut and dried rule in this matter. But generally speaking, to write the kind of book you enjoy yourself is a sound decision.

If you're not sure which choice is best for you, and if you have no special interest in novels, you might try your hand at a nonfiction book first. Your second book could then be a novel. The idea I'm recommending is that you try both sooner or later. This way you'll find out which type you prefer.

What Is Needed to Write a Novel

Here are some of the key things needed to write a novel. A longer list could be presented, but these items are the ones most frequently cited as being very helpful in producing a novel:

- A good idea and the desire to develop it
- The time and freedom
- An intriguing character in some kind of conflict
- A title, theme, mood, or feeling
  Certain observations
  Discipline

Let's look at each of these views on what is needed to produce a novel all your own.

A Good Idea and the Desire to Develop It

There's no guarantee that if you get a good novel idea in your head you're going to actually develop it. Any number of people have thought of good ideas for novels, but they never get around to finishing even the first page.

A good idea, however, plus the desire to develop it can be a strong combination. If the desire to write is there and the idea keeps asking to be developed, this may be enough to get you started.

First novelists can often come up with all sorts of reasons why they shouldn't start work on a novel. The success of the venture depends on how determined the author is.

The Time and Freedom

Who knows how many people from all walks of life have said, "If I only had the time and freedom to write, I'd turn out a hell of a novel!" It's of course one thing to talk about writing a novel and something else to actually do it.

The time and freedom have made it possible for some persons to complete one or more novels. George Sand left her home, husband, and children for the time and freedom to write in Paris. She cared little for her husband, but missed her children terribly.

At first she arranged to spend six months of each year in Paris and the other six back at home. This freedom and time to write encouraged her to develop good work habits early. She had a goal of writing no less than twenty (some reports say thirty) pages each night.

She wouldn't retire for the night until she had finished her regular stint with paper and pen. It was a definite reason for her success and helped a great deal to make her an established author. Her amorous adventures, outspoken opinions, and daring novels (for that era) all combined to make George Sand the talk of Paris before she was thirty.

An Intriguing Character

A character can be so vital that the author is eventually compelled to give him life on paper.

Imagine what it might be like to see and hear a Scarlett O'Hara, Oliver Twist, or Claudius in your mind, to "live with them" as their personalities take shape in your head. Many successful novelists do just that. They live with their characters a long while before getting them into a book. Such an "incubation period" pays off. They often write a stronger, more readable book than they otherwise would.

The Series Character

One way to a fortune as a fiction writer is to develop a series character. Author John MacDonald, for example, created Travis McGee, the hero of more than seventeen crime and suspense novels. MacDonald has turned out over fifty novels at the rate of at least two a year.

Remember Perry Mason? Erle Stanley Gardner did very well with that character, both in books and with a long-running television series.

Edward Aarons created Sam Durell, an intelligence agent, and has published some forty novels (to date) about his adventures.

Once readers get hooked on your character and eager to read more, you can go on turning out new novels for years. And each new book increases your readership and your royalties. Little wonder that a successful series character can be a gold mine for an author; each new book is like another strike coming through for you.

A Title, Theme, Mood, or Feeling

Sources of novel ideas are numerous. Actually, your own life can yield good ideas. Something you read in a book, magazine, or newspaper can set the wheels in motion.

Many authors keep a sharp eye out for those little one or two paragraph stories you see on the back pages of most newspapers. The seeds of some best-selling novels have been found there.

Sometimes all you need is the initial spark or idea association. A title might leap out at you from the printed page or come to you while you're walking the dog or taking a shower.

A feeling you have on a rainy day, a sad, depressed, or happy mood, or even just a phrase may all suggest a possible novel.

Stephen King *(Carrie)* likes to place ordinary persons in unusual situations. He writes to entertain himself, as well as the reader. "The main difference between going to the movies and writing scary books is that you pay to go to the movies. For writing, they pay you."

Some novelists have done very well playing the game of "what if." The idea for *Raise the Titanic* (a big seller) came this way. The author asked an interesting question, "What if someone decided to raise the Titanic?" The book hit the best-seller list fast.

Certain Observations

Gustave Flaubert, the French novelist of the last century, had a special formula for success in writing fiction. As he put it, "observe and then observe again, and again."

Mark Twain wrote about the emotions of people in rural situations and no doubt got many of his initial ideas through observation.

Observations on the good and bad in life can yield all kinds of novel ideas. It paid off handsomely for Jacqueline Susann.

I still remember the first time I stood in Grand Central Station in New York and walked through its enormous main terminal. Thousands of people were passing me on all sides. Many of them had just arrived on a train, while others were hurrying to leave on one, to buy a ticket, or to meet someone else coming into the city.

As I stood there in that busy crossroads of a nation, I thought of the problems which many of those people faced, but also of the happiness, the careers, the challenges, hopes, dreams, and enthusiasm for life itself, which was so evident on many of their faces. Somehow, all of it seemed to crystallize into a key phrase—"a thousand dramas played daily." That's what life is, I thought—a thousand dramas played daily in cities, towns, and villages all over the world.

The phrase which came to me wasn't original. There was a popular radio program many years ago called "Grand Central Station." This was one of the phrases used each time the program started—"a thousand dramas played daily." But the phrase did effectively sum up the life in that busy train station. And key phrases like this can sometimes be the initial spark that leads to a novel.

Discipline

Certainly one of the useful tools for getting a novel (or any book) written is discipline. An author may lack the freedom and time to write, but can still finish one or more novels thanks to the quality of discipline. It's very valuable.

Many fine novels might never be published, if the authors are not willing to pay the price in discipline. Some get up at four or five every morning to finish several new pages of a current work in progress, before going on to a regular eight-hour job. In this way, they eventually complete their books. Others work late at night for one or more years in order to meet their goals.

Think of the discipline of Ernest Hemingway, in his early writing years. He got pitifully small checks from little magazines for years. But he kept at it and eventually became a very successful author—one of the giants of modern literature.

Mary Roberts Rinehart got $34 for her first story. "The checks at first were small, but I was learning a new profession, and I was being paid while I learned. That first year I sold a total of forty-five stories and novellas and earned a total of $1,842.50."

Advantages of Writing a Novel

Most professional novelists have their own list of advantages in writing novels. Some of the direct benefits (to name a few) of novel writing include the following:

1. You gain confidence in yourself, because you actually prove you can do it.

2. You learn firsthand how plot, dialogue, character, and conflict can all work together to produce an intriguing story.

3. You gain experience in telling a story and in how to use fiction techniques, such as the flashback.

4. You find out what type of novel you can write best— especially if you experiment in different categories.

5. You're better able to compare novel writing with nonfiction books, so you can decide which you prefer.

6. The up-front money authors receive for a novel (in the form of an advance against royalties) can often be much larger than the advances for a factual book. This is especially true when paperback companies show interest in the reprint rights to hardcover novels. But the author's reputation and track record have an influence too on the size of the advance. Harold Robbins, for example, can command millions before writing one word.

7. Novels have a better chance of being sold to motion pictures.

Today's Fresh Interest in Novels

Though nonfiction books have held the spotlight for a number of years, novels seem to be making a real comeback. Part of the reason is the fact that more readers wish to escape all kinds of problems including economic worries, pollution, the oil crunch (now affecting many nations), marriage and family troubles, unsatisfying jobs, health problems, and all the rest.

A good novel takes the reader into another world. And, for a change, the reader discovers somebody else's set of problems. Readers still like to read books based on truth, mind you, (meaning nonfiction) but many novels promise escapism and sheer entertainment. Some of these books naturally deliver more effectively on that promise than others.

Types of Novels to Write

If you believe that novel writing is for you, there's an interesting choice available to you. Whether you're a beginner or a veteran, looking over the various types of novels you might write can be helpful. Most of the main categories are included in the following list:

1. Adventure novels
2. Suspense and crime thrillers
3. Gothics
4. Historical romances
5. General romances
6. Mysteries
7. Science fiction novels
8. Occult and supernatural novels
9. Horror novels
10. Juvenile or young adult novels

The above isn't a complete list, but it includes most of the types of novels you might write in the course of a career.

I want to emphasize here that the science fiction novel is in great demand at this writing. The mind-boggling success of the film *Star Wars* and similar series programs on television have sent the sales of this novel category skyrocketing.

While visiting several large bookstores in my area recently, I noticed that there were far more browsers—mostly young people—in the science fiction section than any other. According to reports in the trade publications, this is also happening in many other bookstores in a number of countries. A lot of the sales—for the Saturday afternoon I saw them at least—were apparently science fiction books. This present popularity of science fiction may run its course or continue for some time to come.

One change that seems to be indicated by a number of booksellers—according to a current *Publishers Weekly* survey of 850 book outlets—is a somewhat lesser degree of interest in romance novels. The peak may have been passed for this type of book, though it will continue to sell well. A great many new books in this category appear each year, so the peak of interest was bound to be reached eventually.

Sales for trade paperbacks, regional type books, mass market titles, quality paperbacks, and general hardcover fiction were all reported up (at this writing).

The Gothic

Though current sales of Gothics are waning at present, this type of book is still popular with a great many readers. Women continue to buy this type of book in large numbers.

As in the case of historical romances, women authors often do very well with this type of novel, as you might expect. Such leading Gothic novelists as Phyllis Whitney and Victoria Holt have become millionaires by specializing in this category.

The Gothic novel combines both suspense and romance. The heroine is always a young and attractive woman from about age seventeen to twenty-two or twenty-three. She is quite often forced to take a job as a governess at a large, strange, and somber looking house, which is usually isolated from town.

Coming up with a fresh secret—connected with the house in some way—seems to be the greatest challenge in this kind of novel. Male authors are active in the Gothic field, but they use the pen names of women so they can sell their books. It's still a profitable and fertile book category for women authors. After its appearance in hardcover, a good Gothic can be sold to paperback companies as a reprint and go on to earn extra royalties.

Again, a basic clue as to the type of novel you might do well on may lie in which categories you like to read the most. Until you find the ideal category for yourself, it might be wise to experiment some. You wouldn't have to write an entire book. You could do only a few chapters and then decide whether to complete the project or abandon it for a different kind of novel.

Paul Gallico *(The Snow Goose)* likes to have one novel in the works, one "on the runway," and still another in the "take-off" position.

The Amazing Barbara Cartland

No chapter on novel writing should end without highlighting and saluting the work of Barbara Cartland, known as the queen of romantic novels. Talk about prolific authors! Barbara has written a whopping 222 novels. She once did twenty-two in one year.

Her methods of work are fascinating:

● She talks her novel to a secretary.

● She almost always begins her day's work at 1:00 p.m. and completes up to 7,000 words by 3:30 p.m.

● Before writing word one, she orders her subconscious to come up with a plot.

● She eventually sees her characters in her mind's eye.

● No violence takes place in her books.

● She uses beautiful settings.

● The heroines of her books are virgins. As Barbara puts it, "Purity and innocence are romantic."

● She usually sets her books in the nineteenth century.

So if the romance novel interests you, stock up on some books by this amazing English author. She has style. If anyone has turned novel writing into a sure-fire formula, it's Barbara Cartland. Her methods of working certainly enable her to accomplish a lot.

In the next chapter, we'll take a look at the other end of the book spectrum, that of the nonfiction book.

CHAPTER FOUR

The Wide World of Nonfiction Books

You may well decide to cast your lot with books that are factual. The nonfiction book has great appeal for both new authors and veterans alike. Nonfiction offers you a wide world of writing choices, a veritable supermarket of possible subjects and ideas.

Although the novel makes periodic comebacks in popularity with readers, the nonfiction book remains the favorite type of reading for most of the book-buying public. Sales of books (fiction and nonfiction) at this writing have reached $5 billion and no doubt will continue to rise for the rest of the century. Nonfiction books still account for the largest chunk of this pie.

While there will always be people who buy novels for escape, the majority of book buyers want to read what is true. Self-help books have been quite successful in recent years, along with religious-inspirational titles. Millions of readers everywhere evidently want books that will help them in one or more areas of their daily lives.

The following percentages, compiled by the Association of American Publishers, shows the types of books which have enjoyed the fastest growth in sales from the early to late 1970s:

Mass-market paperbacks—125 percent increase in sales
Mail-order books—92 percent
Professional books—78 percent
Religious books—64 percent
Book clubs—63 percent
College texts—59 percent
Trade books—49 percent
School texts—42 percent
Others—17 percent

Advantages of Nonfiction Over a Novel

Let's examine some of the natural advantages of writing a nonfiction book—over a novel:

• A nonfiction book is usually easier to sell to a publisher.

• Chances are good that you already have some specific knowledge that could be used in a nonfiction book.

• A successful nonfiction book can sell 100,000 copies and higher. If a novel sells 35,000 or 40,000 copies, it's a best seller.

• The odds of writing a nonfiction best seller are more favorable than a novel. The sales of first novels are usually very low (often 5,000 copies or less).

• A wide variety of subjects are available to a nonfiction author.

• A nonfiction book may help many readers in some practical way or teach them, inform them, persuade, entertain, or inspire them. Such books can change lives for the better.

● Nonfiction books often have a longer life in print than many novels.

● What is true is very often much more interesting to read than the product of a novelist's imagination. It's still true that truth is stranger (and often more fascinating) than fiction.

A Nonfiction Book Is Easier to Sell

Generally speaking, it's easier to interest a publisher in a nonfiction book than it is a novel. Why is this so? Simply because a nonfiction book usually means less of a financial risk than a novel.

Publishers as a rule believe in sound business decisions. They're sometimes willing to gamble on novels or uncertain nonfiction books, but most of them can't do it too often. They want to publish books that will earn back their investments and, hopefully, a substantial profit. Too many books on their list that lose money can mean trouble.

Another reason for sticking with the nonfiction book is the time-saving factor. Many publishers require anywhere from three chapters to all of the manuscript of a novel before a decision can be made.

A nonfiction book, however, is often sold on the basis of an outline and one or two chapters. It's obviously far easier to sell an outline and a portion of a book than to complete an entire manuscript on speculation. Nonfiction books are real time-savers in this way.

In the time it would take to write a complete novel and sell it, you could close deals for several nonfiction books and probably even finish the writing on them. It can take years for a novel to make the rounds of publishers before finding a home. These realities are some of the chief reasons that nonfiction authors would rather fight than switch to novels. Nonfiction books have treated them well in the long run.

Your Automatic Credentials for a Nonfiction Book

One clear advantage of doing a work of nonfiction is the credentials you may already have going for you. Dr. Norman Vincent Peale had years of experience behind him as a minister when he sat down to write his best-selling inspirational book, *The Power of Positive Thinking*.

This alone is why there's truth in the belief that there's at least one book in everyone. Maybe not everyone, but certainly a lot of today's busy people, if they could find the time.

The point is that you're bound to have some knowledge, work skills, personal insights, or specialized information that would be of help or interest to others. Search your mind. Clues may lie in hobby interests, civic work you may do, or how you and your spouse saved your marriage. Other topics could include getting ahead of inflation, the right way to vacation in Europe, life in Australia today, your own system for success, camping in Canada, and any number of possibilities.

I'm sure you get the idea. The world is filled with a huge variety of people and no two of them are exactly alike. There are things you can do better than anyone else, and the same is true for your neighbors and other persons you know.

Remember. It isn't a must that you be a recognized authority or expert on a given subject. But any formal credentials will certainly influence a publisher in reaching a favorable decision on your book project. You may have gained specialized information about a subject over the years, in special schools, through on-the-scene-eye-witness experience, or through your own natural talent and observations.

I got hooked on songwriting as a teenager. I stuck with it for a number of years. I filled any number of notebooks with things I learned about the music business. I made the rounds of music publishers in Nashville, New York, and

Hollywood. I was on the scene for many country music festivals in Nashville, and I met songwriters and artists there and at various meetings of the American Society of Composers, Authors, and Publishers (better known as ASCAP).

I learned a lot and, in time, had a number of my own songs recorded and performed in night clubs. Several songs won national awards. During the course of those years, I wrote over a thousand songs.

So when I thought later about writing a nonfiction book, a natural subject for me was a book on songwriting and the thriving music business. And do you know something? I sold this book to the first publisher I submitted it to. The book was published in both hardcover and paperback as *How to Write Songs That Sell*. The book is a backlist title and continues to sell steadily. I believe it will sell for many years to come.

Successful Nonfiction Books Sell Big

Aside from the blockbuster, mass market novels—often paperback reprints from the earlier hardcover editions that sold well—novels as a rule don't sell as well as nonfiction.

Naturally a proven name like Gore Vidal, James Michener, Arthur Hailey, or Helen MacInnes is a guarantee of a big selling novel. But the average novel without a name author behind it doesn't sell nearly as well as the average nonfiction book.

Many publishers are quite happy if some of their novels sell 5,000 copies. If a publisher can get his investment back—plus a small profit—he's often pleased. This is especially true for first novels.

There are occasional exceptions. Sometimes a novel will take off, no matter who wrote it and even though it may be the author's first work.

Nonfiction Books Can Sell Better and Longer

Sam Levenson wrote a book called *Everything But Money*. In its second year of publication, it sold from 2,000 to 4,000 copies a week. Within fifteen months after publication, 310,000 copies had been sold. Sales are much higher today, and it looks like the book will keep on selling in the future.

Some nonfiction books take off like a rocket. In one short week, a Dell paperback, *Our Crowd,* sold a whopping 550,000 copies. And this was before the official publication date of the book.

Some current strong sellers are *The Student Pilot's Flight Manual* (485,000 copies to date), *Be the Person You Were Meant to Be* (670,000 copies), *The Camera Never Blinks* (860,000 copies), *Movies on TV* (875,000 copies), and *The Official Smart Kids/Dumb Parents Joke Book* (305,000 copies).

The Odds Are Better for a Nonfiction Best Seller

Unless you're convinced that you can come up with a mass market novel, your chances of writing a best seller are greater with a nonfiction book.

One good example of a continuously selling book is *How to Get Out of an Unhappy Marriage* (Putnam). This book will no doubt go on selling for some time to come. The market for this book is unlimited. Many a new novel just doesn't have the same staying power.

Look at it this way. As an author, you're more likely to earn a lot of money on a book which can keep selling for years than you would on a title that stops selling in several months or a year. Since you're investing your time and effort in writing new books, why not strive to produce one or more titles that will sell for years to come? It makes good sense.

As you'll realize a bit later in this chapter, you have many interesting nonfiction subjects to write about. Knowing this keeps many authors encouraged and enthusiastic about their work.

If one book doesn't advance toward the best-seller list, another one may do so. In other words, the nonfiction book just seems to offer more potential. On the other hand, how many great novel ideas could you originate?

There are a number of authors who write novels in between nonfiction books. Nonfiction is their bread and butter, and once they discover it they think seriously about switching to a novel.

Such authors, however, will try a novel on occasion, as a change of pace from factual books and to also play an occasional long shot. This method combines both types of writing. The only problem is that many authors can't do both kinds of books; they have to concentrate on one or the other. This is why you should try to find out whether you can write both fiction and nonfiction or if you need to focus on just one kind of book.

A Wide Variety of Subjects

A major appeal of the nonfiction book is the wide subject matter open to you. The choice of subjects for nonfiction books is endless, for example, how to quit smoking, cloning, Jacqueline Onassis, test-tube babies, just to mention a few.

For a good idea of the vast number of subjects available to you, feast your eyes on the following stimulating titles:

The Complete Guide to Eye Care
The Joy of Money
The Adventurer's Guide
The Last Chance Diet
Living and Loving After Divorce

Yoga for Athletics
The Book of Spies and Secret Agents
Pity the Poor Rich
Things to Come for Planet Earth
The Speculator's Handbook
Where Colleges Fail
The People's Almanac
How to Win at Poker
The Lonely Lady of San Clemente
American Caesar
The Great Movie Comedians
Metropolitan Life
The New Money Dynamics
Instant Beauty: The Complete Way to Perfect Makeup
How to Be Your Own Best Friend
The Trouble Book
Meeting of Minds (Steve Allen's book based on his TV
series)
Are You There, God? It's Me, Margaret
The Luck Factor
How to Get the Upper Hand
My 50,000 Year at the Races
RN: The Memoirs of Richard Nixon
The Outlaw Trail (Robert Redford's first book)
Shape Up America
Worlds Before Our Own
Entertaining in Washington
Pulling Your Own Strings
Beyond Death's Door
The Man Who Created Tarzan
The Book of the Back
Pets (Every Owner's Encyclopedia)
There She Is (The Life and Times of Miss America)
Who's Who in Egyptian Mythology
Strike Back at Cancer
The Biggest Tongue-Twister Book in the World

The World's Greatest Rip-Offs
Farm Builder's Handbook
How to Write Songs That Sell (my first book)

Every time you visit a good-sized bookstore, try walking
through the entire store rather quickly. As you do so, let
your eyes glance over the variety of book categories and the
kaleidoscope of subjects available to book buyers. Notice
how many nonfiction titles await a buyer.

I kid you not. If you browse in one or more large
bookstores at least once a week, you're almost certain to
get a good idea of the panoramic array of current nonfiction titles for sale.

And here's the payoff. The many titles that catch your
eye will get your mind into the book groove sooner or
later. Make it a regular habit to browse every week. If you
do this, you'll have new book ideas whispering in your
ears and clicking in your mind pronto.

You'll naturally want to pick up certain books that
interest you. Glance at the jackets, read the copy on them,
look over the contents pages, and maybe read a few pages
here and there. Such a routine, if done consistently, will
help to keep you book oriented.

Actually, bookstore browsing can lead to the marvelous
discovery that you're a potential author. Whether you're a
beginner, a newcomer with little experience, a sometimes
published author, an established professional, or just a
person with general interest in the book field, visiting your
local bookstores can be a real eye-opening practice. It's fun
to know about new books, and it can be profitable for you
in your own writing. Seeing all the fresh books for sale
can increase your desire to write.

After visiting bookstores regularly for some weeks or
months—and of course buying new books that appeal to
you—you should eventually feel a growing desire to write
a book of your own.

Most authors are avid readers. The mere fact that you enjoy browsing in bookstores may be a sign of possible writing ability.

One way to discover your own talents is to wonder what it would be like to visit a local bookstore and see one of your own books on sale. If such a thought fills you with enthusiasm, maybe you should start writing a book. It might just be the start of a wonderful career for you.

CHAPTER FIVE

How to Mine Ideas for Best Sellers

Best sellers are written on all kinds of subjects, so it makes sense to take stock of the variety of book categories open to you. Here are most of the leading ones with examples of titles:

Popular Psychology

1. *Carl Rogers on Personal Power*
2. *Winning*
3. *An End to Innocence (Facing Life Without Illusions)*
4. *Self-Psyching*
5. *The Stress Factor*

Success and Money-Making

1. *National Directory of Income Opportunities*
2. *How to Get the Money You Deserve for Whatever You Want*

3. *Lottery Winners (How They Won and How Winning Changed Their Lives)*
4. *Infinite Riches (Gems From a Lifetime of Reading)*
5. *The Optimist's Guide to Making Money in the 1980s*

Self-Help

1. *The Complete Guide to Eye Care*
2. *Living and Loving After Divorce*
3. *How to Live With and Without Anger*
4. *How to Survive the Loss of a Love*
5. *Successful Financial Planning*

How-To-Do-It

1. *How to Get Control of Your Time and Your Life*
2. *How to Avoid Alimony*
3. *How to Know If You're Really in Love*
4. *How to Advertise Yourself*
5. *How to Write Songs That Sell*

Hobbies, Arts, and Crafts

1. *On Photography*
2. *The Complete Book of Gardening*
3. *Arts and Crafts for Children*
4. *The Complete Book of Drawing and Painting*
5. *Orchids and How to Grow Them*

Cookbooks

1. *The Golden Temple Cookbook*
2. *I Hate to Cook Book*
3. *The Backpacker's Cookbook*
4. *The Cheese Cookbook*
5. *The Fat Counter Cookbook*

Art of Living

1. *Optimism (The Biology of Hope)*
2. *Father to Son: Thoughts to Live By*
3. *Quid: How to Make the Best Decisions of Your Life*
4. *The Art of Problem Solving*
5. *Living Better*

Business and Professional

1. *The Greatest Salespersons (What They Say About Selling)*
2. *The Art of Being a Boss*
3. *Why Managers Fail*
4. *The Investor's Guide to Technical Analysis*
5. *Executive Health*

Travel

1. *The Magic of Ireland*
2. *Switzerland (The Awful Truth)*
3. *Traveler's Joy*
4. *This Is Canada*
5. *Travelability*

Occult

1. *Ritual Magic: An Occult Primer*
2. *Worlds Before Our Own*
3. *Beyond the Four Dimensions*
4. *Mysteries (An Investigation into the Occult, the Paranormal and the Supernatural)*
5. *Questions on Occultism*

Sports

1. *Inside Badminton*

2. *The Poster Book of Horses*
3. *On and Off the Fairway*
4. *Soccer the Way the Pros Play*
5. *The Kentucky Harness Horse*

Religious-Inspirational

1. *Woman Priest*
2. *When Being Jewish Was a Crime*
3. *In Tune With the Infinite*
4. *Spirit-Controlled Family Living*
5. *Love Goes on Forever*

Marriage Books

1. *The Challenge of Marriage*
2. *Closed Marriage: Almost Always You Marry the Right Person*
3. *Husbands and Wives: A Nationwide Survey of Marriage*
4. *The Total Couple*
5. *How to Be Your Own Marriage Counselor*

Health-Physical Fitness

1. *The Drinking Woman*
2. *The Jogger's Book*
3. *Why Your Stomach Hurts (A Handbook of Digestion and Nutrition)*
4. *The Walker's Handbook*
5. *The People's Hospital Book*

Nostalgia

1. *Nostalgia for the Present*
2. *Flashback. The 50s*
3. *James Dean Revisited*

4. *What's My Line? (The Inside History of TV's Most Famous Panel Show)*
5. *The Great Movie Comedians*

History

1. *Who Financed Hitler?*
2. *Illustrated History of the Poles in America*
3. *The Eisenhowers: Reluctant Dynasty*
4. *The Outlaw Trail*
5. *A History of Africa*

Parental-Child Care

1. *How to Protect Your Child Against Crime*
2. *Parents' Guide to Allergy in Children*
3. *Feed Your Kids Right*
4. *The Complete Book of Baby Care*
5. *The Growth of the Child*

Education

1. *Beginner's Guide to Ham Radio*
2. *The New Sex Education: The Sex Educator's Resource Book*
3. *Education and the American Indian*
4. *Overcoming Math Anxiety*
5. *The New York Times Daily Crossword Puzzles*

Communications

1. *Through the Communication Barrier*
2. *Creativity 7*
3. *Communication Arts in the Ancient World*
4. *Women and the News*
5. *Local Radio*

Games-Recreation

1. *The Master's Book of Pool and Billiards*
2. *Precision Bridge for Everyone*
3. *World Chess Championship*
4. *Winning at Casino Gambling*
5. *Greenberg's Operating Instructions and Layout Plans for Lionel Trains*

Music and the Performing Arts

1. *Magic Moments From the Movies*
2. *Costumes for the Stage*
3. *Actress (Postcards From the Road)*
4. *The Lawrence Welk Scrapbook*
5. *Together Again (The Great Movie Teams)*

Exposé

1. *The Anatomy of Arson*
2. *Murder U.S.A. (The Ways We Kill Each Other)*
3. *Child Abuse*
4. *Scandals of '51 (How the Gamblers Almost Killed College Basketball*
5. *The Literacy Hoax (The Decline of Reading, Writing, and Learning in the Public Schools and What We Can Do About It)*

Social Sciences

1. *The American Catholic*
2. *The Population of Israel (Growth, Policy, and Implications)*
3. *A Mediterranean Society*
4. *A History of Sociological Analysis*
5. *The Higher Schooling in the United States*

Science

1. *The Dragons of Eden*
2. *Mind Reach: Scientists Look at Psychic Ability*
3. *Scientists at Work (The Creative Process of Scientific Research*
4. *The Macroscope (A New World Scientific System)*
5. *The Common Sense of Science*

Women's Special Interest

1. *What Every Woman Should Know About Finances*
2. *Surviving Breast Cancer*
3. *Millionairess (Self-Made Women of America)*
4. *Bright Ideas for Your Home*
5. *Fight Back (A Woman's Guide to Self-Defense)*

Sex

1. *The Sexual Connection*
2. *Sexual Shakedown (The Sexual Harassment of Women on the Job)*
3. *The Sex Atlas (A New Illustrated Guide)*
4. *The History of Sexuality (Volume I)*
5. *Sociology of Sex*

Gift Books

1. *The Gold of Friendship*
2. *The Beauty of Motherhood*
3. *God Is Everywhere*
4. *The Joy of Marriage*
5. *Acres of Diamonds*

Juvenile-Young Adult Books

1. *I Shall Not Live in Vain*

2. *Faith of the Presidents*
3. *Straight Talk About Love and Sex for Teenagers*
4. *The Biggest Tongue-Twister Book in the World*
5. *The Boy Who Was Followed Home*

The above list of categories isn't complete. But it gives you a good idea of the variety of subjects open to you. Ideas for books, both nonfiction and fiction, are endless.

But writing a book that may do fairly well is one goal. Creating a best seller is another. Authors have finished their books with just the hope that they might earn enough to justify their time and effort. Some first novelists have been pleased to see their books sell 5,000 to 10,000 copies. Other authors, however, aim higher. They shoot for the best-seller lists every time they start a new book.

There will probably always be some authors who write for the sheer love of books. But most authors write for money. A lot of them dream of their books hitting the *New York Times* best-selling list, being reprinted in paperback for an astronomical figure, and hearing one fine day that Hollywood wants to buy the film rights to their book.

There's nothing wrong with wanting a best seller. It's a worthy goal. One or more best sellers can open the editorial doors of the top publishers and editors in the business. A proven best-selling author like Harold Robbins or James Michener is assured a multi-million dollar advance before the first word of their new books is written. Their previous track records are solid gold.

Timeless Subjects Make Best Sellers

A look at the best-selling titles of today and yesterday reveals a trait shared by many of them—timelessness. They're just as meaningful years later as they were when first published.

Such books as *Life After Life, Treasure Island, The Joy of Cooking, Gone With the Wind, Swiss Family Robinson, Great Expectations, Wuthering Heights, The Death of a President, In Tune With the Infinite,* and many others all have this special quality of timelessness. They'll probably be read hundreds of years from now, assuming that planet earth is still intact.

I challenge you to a test of your own judgment of books. Most publishers announce their new titles twice a year, in the spring and fall. Keep up with these new books, as reported in *Publishers Weekly, Book Digest,* and other leading trade publications.

Then choose the books you feel are most likely to become best sellers. Select them from the titles alone or by looking the books over when they arrive in bookstores.

Here are some sound reasons for conducting such a test:

1. It will show you that a book's timeless quality can help make it a best seller.

2. It helps to develop your judgment.

3. It stimulates your thinking about subject possibilities for your own books.

4. You'll develop a greater awareness of various book categories.

5. It puts you in the editor's or publisher's shoes, by letting you decide which books will become best sellers.

6. It's fun to see how well you did in the test, by comparing your own list of star choices with the sales figures for the books.

7. It keeps you thinking about best sellers in general.

Here's a way you can try your hand now at picking best sellers, without having to wait for the new title announcements of publishers. Some twenty-eight book categories were listed at the beginning of this chapter. Five book titles were given under each category. Almost all of the titles are nonfiction books.

Now here's what to do. Turn back to the start of this chapter and read over the 140 titles of all listed book categories. Then choose the titles of those books which you believe are destined to become best sellers. You may decide only four or five will make it. Or you might list ten or more. Whatever you decide, write down the titles you've selected.

You are only choosing best sellers from a list of titles, but it's still good practice. The whole idea of a book is often reflected in its title. Other titles are not as clear.

Many of the titles listed under the categories were new at the time of this writing. By the time you read this book, however, most of the books will have been in the stores for a number of months. So you'll probably have some clues about a number of them. So don't say I didn't give you any hints.

Keep in mind that some books never become best sellers, even with good reviews and after being publicized quite a bit. Other books take off on their own, without ads or publicity, and sooner or later land on the best-seller charts. This is one reason for the continuing fascination of the book publishing business.

For purposes of this chapter, let's define a best seller as a book that sells 50,000 or more copies, even though many say that a minimum of 40,000 copies sold establishes a book as a best seller. Most of the titles you'll be choosing from are nonfiction, since more nonfiction books are likely to become best sellers than novels. Some fiction titles, however, are included in the list.

Here are the directions again:

1. Turn to the list of 140-book titles given at the beginning of this chapter.

2. Read them over carefully.

3. Choose the titles that you feel will become best sellers. There's no limit to your list, but each one must be a 50,000 copy seller or better to be designated a best seller.

4. If you like, select the titles that you feel will be the poorest sellers.

5. Compare the results of your selections with the actual

sales of the books you listed—as reported in various trade publications like *Publishers Weekly,* which presents a feature in each issue called "Back to Press." (The sales figures of many books that are moving—and on their way to the best-seller lists—are given in this section.)

Assuming that you have a general interest in publishing, you will in time learn if the books you've judged as best sellers actually made it. Another way to find out how a given title is selling is to watch for reports in *American Bookseller* magazine, an important publication for retail booksellers. You can also occasionally check with key people in various bookstores on how a given title is selling. Sometimes it's difficult to get accurate information from booksellers. And of course a book may sell well in one area and poorly in another.

6. Granted that it could take some time to be able to compare your list of titles with the actual sales results of the books, I'm listing my own title choices at the end of this chapter. These are the titles which I personally feel will become best sellers.

So you can compare your list with mine, and then we'll both watch the actual sales of the titles we selected, as they are reported in the months ahead.

If you feel that you want more to go on than just a title, go ahead and buy any of the books listed under the twenty-eight categories. After reading any of them, you may have a better idea of whether the books can sell 50,000 copies. But remember. Just because you enjoy reading a book, your enjoyment is no guarantee that the book will become a best seller.

If you like the best-seller exercise in this chapter, feel free to do the same thing with novels. Make a list of a hundred or more new novels, by referring to the many novel titles found in *Publishers Weekly* and other trade publications. Then study your list and pick the titles you believe will sell at least 40,000 copies (using 40,000 copies as your yardstick for a best seller).

You'll find it harder to judge novel titles, of course, since many of them are not as clear as nonfiction titles. But you can buy some and also read the reviews of many in *Publishers Weekly*.

Some Clues for Spotting Best Sellers

There are pointers for recognizing possible best sellers.

A book that appeals to one or more of the dominant desires of most people has a strong chance of being a best seller. In the same way, when you consider ideas for new books to write yourself, try to focus on a project that will include some of these universal desires of people.

The list below includes twenty-nine of the dominant desires of the masses. Many seek the fulfillment of these desires when they select books, and they can be automatically influenced to buy a book, providing it seems to appeal to some of these ardent desires. Here they are:

To make money
To be praised
To escape physical pain
To attract the opposite sex
To have beautiful possessions
To save money
To be healthy
To be in style
To save time
To be like others
To satisfy one's appetite
To gratify curiosity
To avoid trouble
To be an individual
To be popular
To be self-confident
To be expressive
To have security

To protect one's reputation
To avoid criticism
To take advantage of opportunities
To avoid effort
To have more leisure time
To have prestige
To be comfortable
To advance in social or business life
To have influence over others
To be more creative
To be important

The more of these universal desires which your book promises to fulfill, the better your chances are for a best seller.

From now on, every time you buy, read, or look at a book in a store, think about these dominant desires of people. Ask yourself these three questions:

1. How many dominant wants does this book reflect or offer help in fulfilling?

2. What are the specific dominant wants? Name them.

3. In what manner does the author try to fulfill his promise to the reader?

A key point to remember is that countless millions the world over want to improve their lives in one way or another.

If the books you write can help them to achieve their goals, you've moved a lot closer to the best-seller lists. I'm speaking here mainly of nonfiction books, since it's this type of book that offers practical help and guidance in many cases. Novels are more likely to provide more pure escape for readers. But nonfiction can offer these goodies too.

Some Extra Advice

Here are some extra tips that could be of real help to

you in writing a best-selling book. Refer to them frequently for possible book ideas:

1. Give some thought to the professions. Books with appeal for different professions can stay in print a long time and go through many editions.

2. Reference books earn a lot of money and chalk up excellent sales over a period of time.

3. Almanacs and various directories often do well. *The People's Almanac* and *The Book of Lists* were best sellers and will continue to sell for years.

4. Sales of self-help books are a bit off at this writing, but they're still doing well. This could be the perfect category for your first or next book.

5. Occult books in general haven't been selling quite as well in recent years. But this area is always ripe for a strong new book. If your timing is right, a fresh angle could mean a best seller. *The Search for Bridey Murphy* sold well many years ago. But interest in the occult had not yet been tapped. Many publishers now feel that this category has been somewhat overdone. But the right book could make it big.

6. Many big best sellers are cookbooks. Don't forget this category. If you know this subject, you may have a possible best seller now simmering on your inner stove. Does the world deserve to hear about your special recipes and cooking secrets? If so, the payoff might just be a best seller.

7. Don't rule out the possibility of writing a textbook. There's more work involved than a general trade book but a successful textbook can churn out royalties for twenty to thirty years and longer. One author of a math textbook is reported to have earned over a million dollars from the sale of his book over a period of years.

My Best-Seller Title List

Earlier in this chapter, I promised to list my own selections from the 140 titles given at the beginning of the chapter. These are the titles of those books I personally believe will sell 50,000 copies or more.

See how your own list of titles compares with mine. You'll have to take my word that I haven't read or seen the actual books. I'm deciding solely on the promise reflected by the titles. You'll probably have more to go on, in basing your decisions, since these books will have been out on the market for several months by the time you read this book.

I wish we could sit down and go over our lists together. Only time will tell how we came out and how accurate our best-seller judgment was.

But remember. A number of factors contribute to a best seller. Word of mouth, publicity, advertising, media savvy and promotion, good reviews, the right timing, an attractive cover jacket, a timeless quality, the right breaks, and more.

Both of us might do much better in picking best sellers from the list, by being able to actually read many of the books. A few of the titles are old best sellers.

My objective in devising this exercise for you was to get you thinking more about best sellers in general, the variety of book subjects open to an author, some of the qualities that make a best seller, and the growing realization, which I hope you now have, that you could write a possible best seller. You'll never know unless you try. From the 140 titles, here are my choices. (I picked a lot of them.)

1. *Winning* (Popular Psychology)
2. *The Optimist's Guide to Making Money in the 1980s* (Success)
3. *How to Survive the Loss of a Love* (Self-Help)
4. *How to Know If You're Really in Love* (How-to)
5. *The Complete Book of Drawing and Painting* (Hobbies-Crafts)
6. *The Cheese Cookbook* (Cookbooks)
7. *The Greatest Salespersons (What They Say About Selling)* (Business)

8. *Executive Health* (Business)
9. *Travelability* (Travel)
10. *Worlds Before Our Own* (Occult)
11. *On and Off the Fairway* (Sports)
12. *Soccer the Way the Pros Play* (Sports)
13. *When Being Jewish Was a Crime* (Religious)
14. *Closed Marriage: Almost Always You Marry the Right Person* (Marriage)
15. *The Drinking Woman* (Health-Physical Fitness)
16. *What's My Line? (Inside Story on TV's Most Famous Panel Show* (Nostalgia)
17. *The Outlaw Trail* (History)
18. *Feed Your Kids Right* (Parental-Child Guidance)
19. *Overcoming Math Anxiety* (Educational)
20. *Creativity 7* (Communications)
21. *Winning at Casino Gambling* (Games-Recreation)
22. *Actress* (Performing Arts)
23. *The Literary Hoax* (Exposé)
24. *Surviving Breast Cancer* (Women's Interest)
25. *Sexual Shakedown* (Sex)
26. *The Biggest Tongue Twister Book in the World* (Juvenile-Youth)

CHAPTER SIX

To Outline or Not—
That Is the Question

Whether you write one book or ten, the idea of using an outline is worth some time and thought.

In the case of nonfiction books, most authors find it helpful to make an outline first. For novels, many authors won't use an outline. Others will go to great pains to plan each chapter carefully before writing.

So the basic question of whether or not to use an outline usually depends upon the particular author involved and his or her own feelings about it. Let's look at some of the advantages and disadvantages of using an outline.

An Outline Is a Track to Run On

A sound reason for using an outline is the simple fact that it gives you a track to run on, a road map to follow.

It's often easy to outline an article in your mind. But a book is a much longer piece of work. Books call for a basic plan, a well-organized blueprint showing how you intend to complete the project.

People from all walks of life have remarked on occasion that they could write a book and were going to do it some day. Most of these would-be authors are dreaming out loud. But a number of them would be amazed at the books they could complete, if they would take the time to learn how to do an outline.

An outline is like a series of signposts for an author. It lets him or her see on paper how a book will begin, develop, reach a climax (if a novel), and end. Outlines are like beacons; they light the way for an author when the going may be rough. They steer authors through dangerous waters and help to keep them off the rocks.

A Promising Outline Can Sell Your Book

One of the strongest reasons for doing an outline is because it can help sell your book before you've written a word of it. This is especially true for nonfiction books.

Quite a few nonfiction authors have sold their books to editors based on just an outline and sample chapter. I've done it myself. One of my previous books, on a business subject, was sold from an outline alone.

What this means is that if an outline you create and send to an editor shows enough promise for a finished book, you'll know the happy feeling of receiving an offer for your book.

It's true that many editors will want to see more before reaching a decision—perhaps a chapter or two along with the outline. But never forget that a lot of authors sell their books with just a strong outline. It's being done every day. But your outline must be a good one.

Outlines Grab Attention

A number of authors have been successful at grabbing an editor's attention with an outline. In other words, the author first sends just an outline or maybe a basic description of the project. If and when the editor expresses interest, several sample chapters can be sent. So an outline can be used as a teaser and means of testing an editor's interest.

You'll learn with experience that requirements vary with the editor and publisher. Some editors will make a decision based on an outline alone, particularly if you've had some earlier books published. Other editors need an outline and one or two chapters before reaching a final decision.

If you're new as a writer, with a fear of or dislike for outlines, remember that some kind of plan for your book is probably better than none. And that goes double, if the book you want to write is nonfiction.

An Outline Can Build Enthusiasm

Never underestimate the power of enthusiasm. It can mean a great deal to an author. Staying enthusiastic about your book is vitally important to seeing it through to completion.

Enthusiasm can work like a fuel source. It keeps you hanging-in-there, making decisions, thinking, writing and rewriting, and at your desk continually until your book is finished.

So taking the time and effort to work up a strong outline has a double payoff for you. It gives you a plan for the book and it creates enthusiasm for completing the project.

It may be an old cliché, but it's still very true that man "succeeds by bits and pieces." Most of us need to see the next step in our journey toward a certain goal. An outline shows an author that next step, the next section or chapter to write.

While some authors—including a number of novelists—don't like an outline for various reasons, there are lots of other authors who wouldn't think of writing a book without first creating a sound outline.

What Goes into a Book Outline

Novels—The best outline gives a clear idea of what happens in each chapter of the novel. In this way the entire work can be evaluated and best considered. Some outlines also include the theme and plot, along with a description of the main characters, the conflict of the story, how the complications build to a crisis, resolve in the climax, and how the whole story is brought to an end.

Nonfiction books—A basic statement regarding the purpose of the book can be helpful. Many outlines for this type of book include a table of contents with a description (a paragraph or section subtitles) of what each chapter in the book will cover.

Outlines based on variations of the above descriptions have of course been written and accepted, with or without the editor's request for some sample chapters.

Peter Benchley sold his first novel on the basis of a one-page outline that described his idea for a book about a great white shark that terrorizes a Long Island resort.

Benchley had mentioned this idea to an editor at Doubleday. When the editor asked to see the idea expanded, Benchley described it on paper. Doubleday liked the outline enough to take an option on seeing four chapters.

The eventual book, *Jaws,* was finished nineteen months later and made publishing history. Benchley's total earnings from the book may well reach the staggering sum of $15 million, counting all sources and rights. Quite a jackpot for a first novel.

Length of the Outline

As you've probably guessed, an outline for a book may

run from one to two pages to twenty, thirty, or more. If the outline gets to be too long, it might defeat its purpose.

But the length seems to depend on the particular author and the type of book involved. As a general rule, don't let your outlines run too long. Authors have been known to exhaust themselves on the outline, when it's the book that deserves the bulk of their attention. Don't wear yourself out on the outline so that you have no energy left for the book.

A Word about Book Lengths

Paperback Originals (NOVELS)—Most run from 50,000 to 80,000 words. But adventure books and historical romances may run 100,000 words and over. Saga-type novels tend to run 500 pages and more.

Nonfiction Books—50,000 to 80,000 words in most cases.
Juveniles and Young Adult—Usually about 40,000 to 50,000 words.

Why Many Authors Dislike Outlines

For the other side of the picture, let's take a look at why outlines are disliked by many authors. Some of these reasons are similar to each other. Different authors give their reasons in various ways. In general, here are the reasons why authors turn thumbs down on using an outline:

1. Outlines can be restrictive.
2. Outlines set a limit on the creative process. The author may feel that he or she can't make any changes once the outline has been set.
3. The minds of many authors go blank when they have to make an outline.
4. Authors are often more stimulated by working from an opening sentence, setting, or character introduction.

Harold Robbins rarely if ever uses an outline. He much prefers to type an opening sentence and just go from there.

5. Changes are quite likely to suggest themselves to an author while the actual writing is being done.

6. Many authors simply see little or no use for an outline.

7. Many novelists prefer to "turn a character loose" and see what happens. In other words, they like to discover the story as they write it.

8. "Outlines are flat and cold." A number of authors feel this way and don't mind saying so.

9. An outline may be a poor indicator of the final book. The completed book may turn out far better than the outline suggested. Yet one or more editors may turn the project down, if they don't like the outline.

So an outline may not give an accurate appraisal of the book's style or quality of writing. In short, an outline may be misleading in a number of ways.

10. An author may prefer to work from a simple ABC-outline instead of an elaborate one. A novelist, for example, may require only a basic idea of a story problem and the solution, to produce a worthy novel. An intricate outline may thus hurt the development of a book. The degree to which this is true depends on the particular author involved.

11. Authors have found from experience that an outline of any kind short-circuits their enthusiasm for a book project.

The final decision on outlines is up to you. I want, however, to suggest a method that has worked well for me and might do the same for you. Here it is:

If your book is a novel, don't use an outline.
If your book is nonfiction, use an outline.

Variations on this plan may of course run from a partial outline or working plan—for novels—to a short, medium length, or very elaborate outline for a nonfiction book.

Naturally it helps to know something about your main characters when beginning a novel, along with an idea for the setting. So some degree of planning for a novel is probably a must, whether you put it into a specific outline or not.

You'll have to experiment to see what works best for you. Using an outline for one book doesn't mean that you're stuck with one on all future books. Just go with what each project seems to call for.

Remember that a promising outline for a nonfiction book can go a long way towards selling your project to an editor—before you write the first word of the manuscript. So unless novels are your forte, sound outlines for nonfiction books will probably mean more book sales for you.

Good luck whichever way you go—with or without an outline. You're bound to find out what works best for you through experience. Keep in mind that you can always tear up an outline, change it to please you, or do a brand-new one.

To outline or not to outline? Let it be a new question to answer for each new book.

CHAPTER SEVEN

The First Page Is the Hardest

There's an old saying about marriage you've probably heard many times: "The first fifty years are the hardest!" Well, getting a book underway is a lot easier than getting through even five or more years of married life these days. In the world of books, the first page is often the hardest. Get it done, and you're on your way.

Successful novelist Harold Robbins admits that he prefers to isolate himself when he's working on a new book. But once he gets the first sentence, paragraphs, and page down, he just usually sails through the book.

Maybe it's psychological. But there's something about completing a first page that often sets everything in motion. The inertia against writing has been overcome, and the words start to flow, sometimes like a sweeping tide.

Some authors may get bogged down in those first few pages, but for many, completing the first page acts as a stimulus to continue.

After all, with the first page written, you've proved to yourself that you can make a start on a book.

In other words, for a great many authors, page one has a way of growing into five, ten, or twenty pages. So sooner or later, you realize that those lovely pages have combined to produce a chapter or section of your book. It's a great feeling.

When to Start on Chapter One

Most books—whether novels or nonfiction—require some advance thinking and preparation. Here's a suggested checklist of some things to consider before starting a first chapter. You can use those items that seem right for you:

Nonfiction Books

● Reading, research, and interviews completed. The time needed for research varies from several weeks to years.

● Outline written with all changes to date.

● Sections or subheadings of chapters planned.

● Special anecdotes, examples, and quotes selected for use.

Novels

● Chart or table of characters written, along with a clear description of each (age, appearance, traits, motivations).

● Theme of novel stated in a short and simple sentence.

● Good statement of the conflict of the novel and how it will be resolved.

● Decision made for setting and time of the story.

● Breakdown of the scenes or action of the first chapter or all the chapters. Note: Some novelists plan chapters one at a time, as they come to them. Others block out the entire book. And still others work with no plan at all.

The Challenge of a Blank Page

Some authors are stimulated by a blank page. They warm to the idea of all that white space to be filled with words, sentences, and paragraphs. Other authors may stare in horror for hours or days at the blank page before them.

One person makes an easy start, while another sweats blood. You'll soon discover which type you are. But once writing hooks you, the need to write will drive you, whether it comes easy or not.

Another sign that you may have writing ability lies in this blank white paper. Do you like the feel of it in your hands? If so, it might be a clue.

Even older, established authors with many years of experience behind them still get a thrill from handling blank paper, pens, and pencils, Mystical? Perhaps. Or maybe the sign of a born writer.

What to Do when the Words Won't Come

Some call the refusal of words to come at your bidding an author's block. There may be a valid reason for it including any of the following:

1. You're mentally overworked and have temporarily written yourself out. You've drained yourself and need a rest from putting down words.

2. You're not clear about what you want to say.

3. You're physically exhausted. Trying to think of the right words when you're worn out is fighting a losing battle in most cases.

4. Your body, mind, and spirit are signaling you that they want a change of scenery or some exercise.

5. Worries may be causing a short-circuit. Is your mind on the work at hand?

The work you try to do when you know you're too tired—mentally, physically, or both—is usually a waste

and must be rewritten. So do yourself a favor. Set your
work periods when you're as fresh and in command of
yourself as possible.

Research, Notes, and Quotes Give You Confidence

William Manchester, author of *American Caesar* (a book
on Douglas MacArthur), spent three and one-half years
working on the book. He read a great deal about MacArthur and no doubt had a large amount of research material
ready before starting chapter one.

Collecting the information you need for your book can
do much to provide you with the confidence needed to
make a start. After all, there's the material in front of you
that will make your book come alive. It's in the raw form
of notes, quotes, descriptions, and other material. But it's
there, ready to be whipped into a new book.

In a similar way, the reading and research of a novelist
help to make a certain period of history more real in his or
her mind. So novelists also gain enthusiasm and confidence from their research and it definitely sustains them
when it's time to make a beginning.

One Page Leads to Another

A beautiful thing about writing books, as you'll soon
learn or may already know, is that one page has a way of
leading to another.

Ask any group of authors to name some of the things
they like about their work, and any number will answer
that the piling up of completed pages is one of their
keenest pleasures.

For an author, there's nothing like watching your new
projects grow from just a single page to hundreds of
pages. Best-selling author William Buckley, Jr. says it this
way: "I get pleasure out of having written. I like to paint.

I don't like writing, but there is a net satisfaction when it's done. I write every day without excuse. If you put in seven days a week at 1500 words a day, in five weeks you have a book.''

It's true that the piling up of pages may be a bit harder if it's a first book. But many authors agree that the more experience you gain, the easier the writing becomes. Some books are naturally tougher to write than others, depending on the scope of the subject and its development.

Take Advantage of Cycles

After you've gained some degree of experience, you'll realize that your productivity runs in cycles. There are periods of time when the words just seem to flow. Every author learns how to recognize these cycles and to shift into high gear at such times when the creative juices are flowing so as to use the high point in the cycle to maximum advantage. You should plan to do the same.

In time, you'll be able to anticipate these fortunate upswings and know in advance when one is about to begin or end.

So be ready to hit your stride at such periods and get in as much time at your work as possible. You can often double or triple your output during these highly creative periods. They're like velvet clearings you reach in the forest. Use them wisely.

Promise Yourself Little Rewards

Lots of smart authors get more work accomplished, or simply make their current projects go more smoothly, by treating themselves to little rewards now and then.

These small rewards vary from taking a ten minute break, after finishing several pages or a certain segment of work, to relaxing in front of the television set for a while.

One author may take a day off, after completing a chapter. Another will spice up his work day with short coke or coffee breaks. Some authors work like beavers Monday through Friday and then relax over the weekend. Others seem to work in spurts and then knock off for a day or so.

There are plenty of authors who almost never quit. They're working all the time; if they're not writing they're involved in research, interviewing, planning, or some other work-related activity.

Someone once wrote that "the true author works constantly throughout his or her career." In the sense that most authors think about their work a great deal, even when actively engaged in some other activity, this is very true.

Real authors can't seem to shut it off. The process is going on within them constantly. A great many authors seem to be happiest when they're working on books. Some authors achieve money and success enough to relax a bit but continue writing for its own sake.

Some authors say they experience a terrible let-down after a book is completed. It's a trying time for such authors. They're a bit depressed when the work on one project comes to an end and they're ready and anxious to get on with their next book.

Work Methods of Some Famous Authors

JOHN O'HARA—He was a night author. He wrote many of his best-selling novels in the small hours of the morning.

HAROLD ROBBINS—The first sentence seems to get him going. He just writes from that point on, discovering the characters and story as he goes.

TAYLOR CALDWELL—She usually works from midnight to dawn. Once she gets started, she doesn't stop writing until what she has in mind for that work session has been completed to her satisfaction. Taylor does a lot of research and travel. She may at times destroy entire pages or rewrite them a number of times.

ARTHUR HAILEY—Research usually keeps him busy for a full year, followed by another period of up to six months on an outline, which is an extensive one running from forty to fifty pages. About eighteen months is devoted to the actual writing. Hailey writes first in longhand and then types the material. His daily word goal is just 600 words, but he may rewrite some paragraphs from this work four or five times.

REX STOUT—This author of many detective books likes to begin a new book on the tenth or twelfth of January, completing the project in forty days. All he usually starts with are the names of the characters, what they do, and what their ages are. "That's all the outline I have."

NORAH LOFTS—She puts in a long day at her writing desk, working from 9 a.m. till 1 and then 4:30 till 7:30. She sticks to this schedule just about every day, year after year.

STEVE ALLEN—This talented author seems to thrive on variety. Along with books, he writes songs, short stories, and television programs. He reads fast and likes to dictate notes into a small hand tape recorder. Allen stays well organized. He currently has a list in his office with more than twenty future book projects planned.

CHAPTER EIGHT

Chapters Make Your Book

It may sound a bit obvious, but try to keep one fact about writing books in the forefront of your mind at all times: Chapters make your book. This basic truth can help you finish any number of books.

Chapters make up the framework of your book. One chapter doesn't make a book. Most books have at least ten chapters, and a vast number of books run twenty or more chapters.

You can sustain your enthusiasm for a book by realizing that you draw ever nearer to its completion with every new chapter you finish.

Don't underestimate the strength behind the truth. Many people who consider writing a book never actually do it. An important reason they never do, is that the thought of all the work involved scares them.

It can be frightening to think of the work required for a book, regardless of the length.

So don't do it. Don't let your book project as a whole leer at you with its length, scope, or amount of work needed to become a reality. Seeing all that work—in one massive dose—can depress even the best of authors.

Your salvation as an author lies in chapters. By breaking the total book down into chapters, you're not overwhelmed by the sheer magnitude of it. You may not be able to see how your book will end, or even the middle part of it. If not, don't worry about it. Just concentrate on doing one chapter at a time.

Give your attention to the chapter at hand. When you're satisfied with one chapter, move on to the next one. You'd be surprised how many books get written in this way. Chapters have a marvelous way of adding up just like pages do.

Focus on the bits and pieces of your book, namely the words, sentences, paragraphs, pages, and chapters. These will all work together to produce the beginning, middle, and ending of your book.

This important truth about writing books can do much to help you finish your first book, and go on to a second and third one. Look at it this way. If you wrote just one page a day for the next year, you'd have a completed book of 365 pages. Or you could do the same by writing two pages a day for six months. The work schedule you set and stick to is up to you.

Planning Chapters in Advance Pays Off

Some authors develop any number of ways to keep making progress on their books. One author, for example, plans his next chapter whenever he finds himself bogged down with a current chapter. This way he doesn't lose valuable time.

A lot of professional authors work hard on the advance planning of chapters. Such work pays off when they're ready to begin the actual writing of a book. After you complete chapter one, you already have a plan for chapter two and know where you're heading with the material. The reason is that advance planning has been done. This keeps the progress of your book moving forward smoothly but continually.

Advance planning of chapters can be another source of enthusiasm for you. You're eager to get into the next chapter of your book, because the plan for it is ready and waiting. The total effort results in increased confidence as your book comes to life.

Chapter Headings Stimulate Your Writing

While it's true that some novels don't have any chapter headings, most nonfiction books make use of them.

Chapter headings can even increase the sales of your book. Watch how many browsers and customers in bookstores skim through books glancing at the chapter headings. Many will decide to buy a particular book, if the chapter headings offer promise of good reading.

What's more important is the fact that well-written chapter headings stimulate your writing all the way through your book. Some of them will interest you more than others, but all of them act as signals. They tell you what each chapter is about and what the reader is likely to find there.

Vary the Length of Your Chapters

Never forget that all readers are human. Give them some variety in the length of your chapters. Don't follow one long chapter with too many others of the same length. Break the pace with a short chapter now and then.

If properly placed in a book, short chapters provide relief and help the reader to feel that he or she is making progress in getting through the book. No reader likes to feel that it's a chore to finish a book. In other words, make the reading journey as easy and clear as possible.

A number of readers often take a rest or refreshment break after finishing a certain number of chapters. If many of your chapters are too long, the readers may have to stop in the middle or end of a page in order to take their breaks.

Most people enjoy variety in the books they read. No author can ever be certain that those who buy his or her book will read it straight through at one sitting. It's nice to at least think that some might do so. But reading habits along with comprehension levels differ. So help the reader along with variety in your chapter length, style, and presentation.

Some Chapters Are Tougher Than Others

Any author worth his or her salt knows from experience that some chapters are harder to write than others. It's just par for the course.

Whether you write one book or twenty, you'll soon discover this fact for yourself. Some chapters almost write themselves. The work seems to flow. The material seems fresh and vibrant. The author is enthusiastic and may even feel sorry to reach the end of such chapters.

Not so with other chapters. An author may get stuck at any point in more difficult chapters. If and when this happens to you, don't force it. If you get bogged down, try one of the following remedies:

1. Take a break. Relax and think about something else for a while. You'll come back refreshed and better able to solve the problem.

2. Liquid refreshment may help. Drink a coke, cup of coffee, tea, or glass of fruit juice. Nothing stronger. Remember. You're writing. Liquor and writing don't mix well for most authors.

3. Take a brisk walk for thirty minutes or so.

4. Try reading the material out loud. This can sometimes help to point the way forward.

5. If nothing seems to work, it might be best to knock off work for a few hours or even until the next day.

Once they have their book outlines, some professional authors go through them and mark the chapters they feel will be most interesting or easiest to write and those which will be the toughest.

Then they can alternate between difficult types of writing—first completing an easy or interesting chapter followed by a tougher one. Some authors of course find every chapter hard to write. And still others, the lucky ones, enjoy working on every single chapter in their books.

Chapter One Sets the Theme of Your Book

I hope you already realize the importance of a first chapter. This is your grand opening. The spotlight is on your beginning sentences. The reader's attention is focused on your words.

In the case of novels, the first few paragraphs may well determine whether your book is bought. Many a prospective buyer of your book will read the first page before making a decision to buy or place your book back on the shelf.

So the opening paragraph should be strong enough to grab the reader's attention and say: "Hey, there, you with the bloodshot eyes. Buy me. I'm good reading. You won't be able to put me down."

Prospective nonfiction book buyers may read half or more of the first chapter, before deciding whether or not to buy. This is especially true if the opening chapter is fairly short.

So the first chapter often influences a buying decision.

Don't underestimate the pulling power of this starting chapter. It also sets the tone and establishes a theme, or purpose of your book.

If sent with an outline to an editor, your first chapter can mean the difference between the sale of your book or its prompt return to you. No wonder many authors rewrite their first chapters several times. They know it's that important.

Make Your Last Chapter as Good as the First

Some authors are so glad to reach the last chapter in their books that they're tempted to rush through it as quickly as possible. To do so is a mistake.

A sound rule for writing books that will sell is to do all in your power to make your last chapter just as strong as the opening one. Actually, this rule should apply to every chapter in your book.

Do your best on every chapter, and you'll never feel sorry later that you didn't give a particular chapter your best effort.

Remember, it's too late after your book is in print. You won't be able to make changes or rewrite paragraphs. When your book comes out, that's it, until a future edition, if any, is published. That may never happen.

So do your level best all the way through your book. Then you can know that you did all you possibly could to write an effective and worthwhile book.

Then, whether your book sells 5,000 copies or 100,000, you'll be proud in the knowledge that you gave your all to the project. Who could ask for anything more?

CHAPTER NINE

Getting Along with Editors

Since so many books are sold these days from an outline—or before a word of the manuscript is on paper—it's not too early to discuss the matter of getting along with editors.

Even on book sales which involve a chapter or two and an outline, most of the manuscript is yet to be written. In other words, many an author wisely attempts to sell his or her book to an editor before very much of the manuscript is completed. So knowing how to get along with editors can be vital to your success.

This chapter is meant to save you time, misunderstanding, frustration, and money in dealing with various editors. Much of the information is based on direct experiences I've had with many editors myself over a period of several years. There are good and poor editors, responsible and careless ones, courteous and rude ones, and professional and not-so-professional ones.

Whether you write novels or nonfiction, you'll have to deal with editors until the day you get an agent. Some authors prefer by choice not to use an agent, because they like to deal with editors themselves. There's an awful lot to be said for knowing what's going on with your various book projects. Direct communication with editors makes that possible and often sooner than with agents.

Perhaps the best way to view the editor's role in the book publishing business is to understand that editors are the gate-keepers of the industry. They decide what will be accepted and published.

Many authors, however, have done well using an agent to represent them. There are advantages and disadvantages to either choice. The best advice I can give you about agents is to check them out carefully before signing up as a client. Trust is vital in the author-agent relationship. The wrong agent can be a drag to your writing and short-circuit the success you want.

In most cases, an agent won't even consider taking you on as a client until you've had one or more books published. So you'll be representing yourself, in the beginning at least.

Here are a number of important realities about editors that you need to be aware of for better overall results in working with them:

● Most editors are looking for new books.

● Many editors move around frequently from publisher to publisher. They want to know they're advancing in their careers and try to do just that with each move.

● Generally speaking, editors earn less money than agents. A number of editors resent this fact. They have to deal with agents, but some are sensitive to the fact that agents earn more than they do.

● Editors appreciate receiving a query letter describing a book project before the proposal or manuscript is sent. This saves both the editor's and author's time. If the project doesn't sound right to an editor, the author saves time, postage, and wear and tear on the material. Professional editors do appreciate any author who saves their time, which runs out all too quickly every day.

● Some editors don't like simultaneous submissions. Others will consider them with interest. So find out first by letter or market study if a particular editor will look at a project that's also being sent to several other publishers.

● The large majority of book editors are overworked. There just aren't enough hours in the day for all their various duties, decisions, meetings, correspondence, and other functions. Show that you understand this, and many editors will remember you favorably.

● Most editors are professionals. But there are some who are incompetent. Here are some clues that you should be alert to when dealing with editors. They may signal the signs of an unprofessional editor:

1. He or she fails to reply to your letters (assuming your letters are neat, businesslike, and professionally typed).

2. He or she holds book projects for unreasonably long periods with no explanation as to what's going on. In my early eareer as an author, I once waited a solid year for a decision from a New York publisher. My letters requesting some word on the book project were all ignored.

Mark this well. Life is too short. Never let an editor or publisher treat you like this. There are too many professional editors who will give you prompt and courteous decisions regarding your material. Whenever you run into an editor or publisher who will not, just cross him or her off your list.

My last two books were accepted within two weeks. Believe me when I tell you that there are many editors and publishers who will treat you well.

3. He or she says one thing in a letter or by telephone and then does just the opposite. Apparently some editors will say anything in a letter and then later contradict themselves.

4. He or she expresses strong enthusiasm in seeing any new book projects, but then finds something wrong with every one over a period of time. This could be a sign that such an editor is simply "shopping around." Or perhaps such editors want to pass worthy ideas along to their pet authors.

5. He or she accepts a book, offers you a hefty advance, holds the manuscript for three months or longer, doesn't send a contract, and then finally cancels the whole deal. This once happened to me with a major New York publisher. And I've been wary of certain publishers and editors ever since.

6. He or she fails to respond to ideas for new books. This is supposed to be a key function of an editor, but it's evidently one of the first things some of them forget. Don't waste your time with such editors. There are plenty of other editors who will gladly respond to your new book ideas.

7. He or she is rude or discourteous.

• Some editors swing more weight in their companies than others. The best editors are those who believe in you and your book, go to bat for it in important meetings, and take an active interest in it all along the way.

Such editors do much to make a book successful. They can keep a book alive, see that it isn't overlooked or lost in the shuffle, and keep the marketing and sales teams enthusiastic about it. There aren't enough of such editors around. It's a great day when an author finds such a good editor.

• Editors can and do make big mistakes. Don't ever forget it. Some of the most successful books of all times were turned down by any number of editors. The quality of judgment of some editors is head and shoulders above that of their colleagues.

• A number of editors in the business are frustrated authors.

• Some editors act like they're doing an author a great

favor to communicate in any way. Get away from this kind of editor fast. Book publishing is built on communication, from the initial spark of an author's idea to the bound, published books and sales-promotion push behind them.

● It's very difficult to become friends with some editors. Don't go out on a limb to be friendly. You may get chopped off quickly. Strive to be as businesslike as possible. Let the editor make the move toward the two of you becoming friends. Since they deal with each other for years, some editors and authors do become friends.

A major reason that certain authors stick with the same publisher for many years is because of a lasting friendship with an editor. The legendary friendship of Thomas Wolfe and Max Perkins is an example. Some editors and authors just seem to hit it off from the start and work well as a team. The result is many a fine book.

● Most editors have a built-in sense of fairness regarding advances on accepted books. You may become a valuable author in time, and they know it. Some authors without agents claim they can do as well—or close to it—in negotiations with editors on advances.

● Editors will often give an agent a much quicker decision on a book project than an author without an agent. Some agents brag that they can get a decision within days. Usually, if a book is really good, you can get a quick decision on it yourself, direct from an editor.

● If an editor you're dealing with has confidence in you and your future prospects as an author, he or she may be very willing to offer a two- or three-book contract. This happened some years ago between McGraw-Hill and Clifford Irving. He got a four-book contract and an advance of $68,000 out of a total of $150,000 to be paid over a four-year delivery period. So always keep the possibility of a multi-book contract in mind.

● Some editors will make a decision based only on a

complete manuscript. This is often true in the case of novels. So you must decide whether to finish a manuscript on speculation or try another editor who is willing to give you a decision based on an outline and a chapter or two.

● It's usually unwise to use salesmanship on editors. They know what they want and will usually disbelieve any statements that what you've sent them is a sure best seller. It's okay to be enthusiastic about a project, but don't overdo it until there's some sign that your editor agrees with you. Your work will speak for itself in most cases.

● If you don't like certain clauses in various book contracts offered to you, negotiate with the editor for a better deal. Most contracts are negotiable.

● Don't automatically blame the editor if your manuscript comes back without the postage you enclosed and you end up having to pay the postman. It happens frequently to authors. Editors are not usually to blame. The fault may lie with the employees in the mail room.

● Editors read widely. They know about fads, world events, politics, and what's going on in many places.

● Editors regularly scan a variety of magazines and newspapers, watch reviews, keep up with theater, television, radio, college writing, plus new books of other publishers. Many editors always keep an eye out for new writing talent wherever they can find it.

A few years back, an occult article I'd written was published in a national weekly newspaper. Two New York editors saw the article and contacted me about doing a book on the occult. So keep in mind that anything you write that's published may catch the attention of a book editor.

● The best editors not only discover new authors; they also encourage and nurture them over a period of time.

● When and if an editor fails to react to an idea you send for a book, cross him or her off your list. There's no excuse for not responding to your letter. I personally have no respect for such editors. And you shouldn't either. A professional editor keeps an open door to all with new ideas. And good book ideas may come from anyone.

• Many editors have a tendency to label authors as "argumentative," "stubborn," "professional," "uncooperative," "impatient," or some other designation.

Editors also claim that certain authors have enormous egos, which must be tended to carefully. But it works both ways. Some editors have gigantic egos themselves and sometimes show little appreciation or respect for an author's time. Some editors demand professionalism from authors, but often fail to show any themselves.

If you should find on occasion that you can't work with a particular editor—no matter what—break off the connection and seek a new editorial contact. Watch the trade papers and especially *Publishers Weekly* for the names of new editors you can try.

• Editors frequently get ideas for new books themselves and then try to find the right authors for those subjects. So after you get to know an editor, let him or her know that you'd like to be considered for new book projects originated by the editor.

• The majority of recognized authors use an agent today. But many editors have no objection at all to communicating directly with an author. A full 90 percent of the editors I've dealt with have been very fair, courteous, and professional in every way. As for the remaining 10 percent, the only thing an author can do is realize that every industry has its share of bad apples. When the signs are clear that you've run into one of these editors, sever all ties.

And when you're lucky enough to work with one of the many fine editors in the book business, do everything in your power to cooperate with him or her. A good editor to work with—one who believes in you and your books—is of prime importance for lasting success.

You might well say that for an author, happiness is a good editor to work with. When you find such an editor, stick to him or her like glue; such an editor can help you achieve great success.

CHAPTER TEN

How to Test Your Book before You Write It

Back in Chapter 6, the question of whether or not to make an outline for a book was discussed. There's another important question you'd be wise to ponder every time you have a new book project in mind: Should you query a publisher first to see if your idea is of interest?

Since the time of most good editors is short, a strong case can be made for sending a query letter first regarding a new book idea. Editors appreciate it and will be able to get back to you quicker because of it.

The query letter has grown in importance considerably in recent years. Many editors of books, magazines, and newspapers list a preliminary query letter as a definite requirement for doing business with them.

The beauty of the query letter is that it lets you sell your book before it's even written. A query letter hits the editor with your basic book idea. And if the editor likes the sound of the idea, he or she will want to see more.

A query letter also gives an editor an idea of your writing style, shows your thoughts about the subject of the book and provides hints as to whether your basic idea and choice of subject indicate a worthwhile book. A good query letter can convince an editor that you have what it takes to complete a book.

It makes sense to find out if a new book idea hits an editor right or not. Many publishers have developed a certain type of book list over the years. So a cookbook, for example, or title on investing, or any number of other subjects may be completely wrong for a given publisher.

So the author saves his or her own time and the editor's too, by first sending a query letter to sound out an editor on a new idea.

You'd be surprised how many authors and would-be authors send off their manuscripts to publishers with no knowledge of what a particular company specializes in. Cookbooks shouldn't be sent to a publisher of detective novels. Religious books sometimes arrive in the offices of a craft or gardening type publisher.

A go-ahead response to a preliminary query letter is no guarantee of an acceptance by an editor. But it does often signal an editor's interest in your idea and possible desire to see an outline and a few sample chapters.

Hit Them with an Idea First

Now let's assume that you've come up with a new book idea. You like it and believe it would sell. How do you present your idea to publishers? Here are some choices open to you:

● Describe your idea briefly in a letter (a few paragraphs to a full page).

● Give a clearer description in about a two-page letter.

● Describe your idea in a letter to a dozen publishers and offer to send an outline and sample chapter. This is the multiple submission method. Numerous authors report good results from using it. You can of course send multiple query letters and also multiple outlines and chapters to a dozen or more publishers.

● Hit the editor you write or phone with a working title. This can help the book idea to jell better in the editor's mind.

● Simply state that you want to write a book on a given subject and tell why you believe it might be right for that publisher. Do this for each company you contact.

● Ask the editor if he or she is currently interested in new book projects. Name the categories that include your book ideas such as self-help, children's books, adventure novels, or whatever.

This last method is really just a request for an editor's okay to send some new book projects. It can sometimes work if your timing is right. An editor may well be looking for some new titles in certain categories like health or popular psychology, for example, so you might get a green light to send what you have in those categories.

Most editors discover through experience that good publishing ideas come from virtually everywhere. A taxi driver once made an interesting remark to a Harper and Row editor: "I wish someone would write a book describing a thousand ways to amuse a child."

Harper and Row's policy at the time was to pay $100 to anyone who suggested a book idea which they accepted. A bit later, Harper published a book based on the driver's idea: *838 Ways to Amuse a Child.* The book did well and sold for many years.

Good Idea but the Wrong Publisher

This can and does happen to many authors. Some authors with lots of experience still find it difficult at times to remember which publishers do certain types of books. With over 1100 book publishers currently in the United

States alone, it can be a real task to remember who wants what type of book.

A good way to handle this matching of a book idea with the right publisher is to request the latest catalogs from publishers. After studying these catalogs, pick the companies you believe you'll have a realistic chance of selling.

Remember that the titles listed in a catalog may not currently be what an editor wants. Maybe they've decided to change their line of books. So ask the editor if the books listed in their catalog are a good indication of what they want.

A few years back, I sent a major publisher a general nonfiction book project. I'd had some earlier correspondence with the editor, and he'd given me his okay to send any new projects I thought might be right.

In a few weeks, I received a very nice letter from the editor. He called the detailed outline and chapters I'd sent on the project "a model plan for a book." Unfortunately, his company did not publish books on that particular subject, which was marriage.

If I had checked on their subject limits before sending the project to him, I would've known that they were the wrong publisher for that book.

So try to send your new ideas and book projects to the right publishers. This right matching can increase your number of sales. A large percentage of rejections are the result of an author sending his proposal to the wrong company.

The Advantage of a Strong Title

Never underestimate the power of a strong title for a book. Editors respond to titles that hit them favorably. Here are a few examples from books that chalked up many sales. Some of them are still selling at this writing and may do so for years to come:

Everything You Always Wanted to Know About Sex

God Is for Real, Man
You Were Born on a Rotten Day
Learning to Love Again
The Joy of Cooking
How to Write Songs That Sell (one of my own books)
Dress for Success
The Last Chance Diet
Raise the Titanic
How to Fix Damn Near Everything
If Life Is Just a Bowl of Cherries, What Am I Doing in the
    Pits?

Length of a Query Letter

In most cases, a one-page letter will be enough to describe your book idea and to suggest a few working titles. It's probably better not to take more than two pages to tell what you have in mind.

In my own case, most of the query letters I've sent to editors have consisted of not over one page (typed single-space). A long letter—more than two pages—is no guarantee of a go-ahead from an editor. It's what you say and the promising quality of your idea that count the most.

The Practical Way to Sell Your Book

I can't repeat one bit of advice too often: Don't write a complete manuscript unless you have the time and are willing to gamble on a finished manuscript. Describe your book idea first to some editors and get their reactions. If they like your idea, they'll ask to see more. Then you can send an outline and a sample chapter or two.

Why spend the amount of time and effort necessary to do a complete manuscript, unless you have a firm commitment from a publisher in the form of a contract and advance? Some authors do write a complete book and then try to sell it.

But believe me. Many professional book authors test ideas first and then sell editors on an outline and a few chapters. This is the most practical way to sell your book projects today.

If your book is a novel, you may well have to write a good portion of it before an editor will give you a decision. Publishers vary on how much material they need to see from a novel. Some will decide on three chapters and an outline. Others prefer a complete manuscript. So find out first what a particular publisher requires.

It's hard for many authors to work on a complete manuscript without worrying most of the time if it will sell when finished. It's very nice to know that the manuscript you're working on each day has already been sold. You have a signed contract and hopefully an advance. You then have no doubts that it will sell. You have the assurance of knowing it's going to be published, unless you fail to do a good job on the rest of the book.

Bertrand Russell, the English philosopher, said it well: "Worry is a form of fear, and all forms of fear produce fatigue. One who has learned not to feel fear will find the fatigue of daily life enormously diminished."

With time and some experience behind you, I think you'll come to appreciate the wisdom of testing and selling a book project before writing the complete manuscript. That's the way the pros do it.

CHAPTER ELEVEN

Pros and Cons on Agents

Author Judith Guest got her first novel published without the services of an agent. Her first book, *Ordinary People*, enjoyed enormous success.

It frankly puzzles me why people are often amazed when an author sells his or her book without an agent. It happens every day.

Agents are not gods with magic wands. If a book project of yours is worthy of being published, you can place it yourself with some persistence and confidence. If it's not up to par, you won't be able to sell it and neither would an agent.

Several years back, *Publishers Weekly* reported on an author who tried three different agents. Not one of them got her a book contract or even a magazine article sale. One of the agents she tried lost some of her articles and did absolutely nothing to collect the 10 percent royalties on a book she sold herself.

Her reaction to this unhappy experience with three different agents is worth remembering. Her advice to authors is frank: "You shouldn't try to get an agent. There isn't 10 percent of difference between what you can get and what an agent can get for you." Many, however, would disagree with this assessment.

Some authors with little confidence in agents have handled the contract details and rights to their books themselves and have done well at it. Others have no doubt come out on the short end of the stick.

Let me assure you that many authors have profited considerably through the services of a reliable and competent agent. The right agent can definitely be a real help to you. The wrong one can actually hurt your chances for success.

Here are some of the advantages of being represented by an agent. When you reach the point in your writing that you feel the need of an agent, you can weigh both sides of the question before arriving at a decision. Here they are:

Advantages of Having an Agent

1. A strong agent can often get a larger advance than you could get dealing directly with an editor. This isn't always true. It depends on a number of things such as your name value (if any), previous successes, the type of book project, and other factors.

It's true that some smart authors do well acting as their own agents. Some are better horse traders than others.

2. A good agent can be of great help in the area of foreign rights. Many agents have branch offices or representatives overseas to handle such business. An alert publisher, however, can often take care of foreign rights for you. It can mean extra money for them, too, so they're not likely to overlook or mishandle this source of extra revenue.

3. An agent relieves the author of the business details of his or her writing. This means that an author can focus on writing and not have to worry about contracts, subsidiary rights, copyrights, escalating royalty clauses, and so on. An agent takes care of it all. But for this very reason, you'd better have a trustworthy relationship with your agent.

Donald MacCampbell, a highly successful New York agent who has sold more book properties than any other living agent, advises authors in his book, *The Writing Business*, to personally meet an agent before signing up as a client: "You must try to meet an agent in person before you become involved, so that together you can assess the likelihood of a long-term relationship. It is very much the same as entering a marriage: you do not have to be in love, but you had better be damn good friends."

4. If you intend to publish a number of books in the years ahead; the services of an agent are practically a must. You could possibly lose a good deal of money by trying to handle everything yourself. However, if you plan only a few books, you could probably handle things yourself. In any case, most agents won't take on new clients, until they've attained some success.

5. Agents can sometimes show an author how to rewrite a project or book outline so it will be accepted instead of rejected.

6. If your books are mostly novels, the better agents are equipped to negotiate the film rights for you on any sales to Hollywood. A number of agents have representatives on the west coast.

7. The author-agent relationship can grow into a lasting friendship. An agent shouldn't be expected to be a nursemaid to an author, but it helps many authors to know that he or she isn't alone, that an agent cares and is pulling for the author.

8. Some agents allow their clients to call them on the phone to discuss various problems.

Scott Meredith, another highly successful New York agent, truly likes his authors. He gives his home telephone number to each new client and receives calls from some of his authors in the middle of the night. Like Donald MacCampbell, Meredith is also an author. He started writing at age fourteen.

Meredith sold 7400 properties last year and earns in the neighborhood of $300,000 a year after taxes.

Here's something worth noting about both MacCampbell and Meredith as agents. Both have solid reputations for responding promptly to authors. Some agents sit on letters from authors for weeks and months. Both MacCampbell and Meredith reply in several days.

9. A respected agent in the business can often get much quicker decisions on book proposals and outines, as well as faster readings on complete manuscripts. Some agents claim they can get an initial reaction within forty-eight hours and a decision for an author within days, depending on the nature of the book.

Dealing directly with editors may take from two months to over a year, unless you have a successful track record to point to. So some authors rightfully feel they may be old and gray by the time their book has made the rounds of the leading publishers. An agent can thus save you months or years of time. And remember. Time is the most valuable commodity an author has.

According to Ann Elmo, "A submission by an agent gets faster action by an editor. As to a reply from an editor, the proposal takes less time, of course—about a week or ten days."

10. A good agent can be a vital link in matching the right author with the right editor.

11. In addition to books, some agents will also sell other material written by an author including articles, motion picture screenplays, television scripts, and other literary properties.

Disadvantages of an Agent

1. An agent takes 10 percent of your advance and 10 percent of the royalties from book sales. Some authors prefer to keep all the money themselves.

2. A great many authors, if not most of them, are located outside of New York City. Being "out in the hinterlands" makes some authors feel isolated and they are concerned that an agent might favor in-town, on-the-scene authors. This is also true for authors overseas who live outside London, Paris, and other literary centers of the world.

Other out-of-town authors believe that their work gets shuffled aside because of their home base. Whether this is true or not, authors worry about it.

3. Some agents fail to communicate promptly with authors. I once sent one of my very best book projects to a New York agent, after getting written permission to do so. I was patient for six weeks. I felt that some kind of response from the agent should've been sent to me within six or seven weeks.

I later asked for the return of my material and had to wait several more weeks before the agent sent it back. I suspect that the project sat in a file on the agent's desk. Some agents like to screen what various authors are writing and have no intention of trying to sell it.

Just like some editors, there are agents who sit too long on projects sent. Authors shouldn't expect replies from agents within days or immediate action on all matters. An agent may have fifty, one hundred, or five hundred other clients. But I think that an author deserves some initial reply regarding a project within six to eight weeks, even if it's only an acknowledgment that the material arrived safely. The better agents reply much faster.

4. It's difficult for an out-of-town author to know who the most reliable agents are. It's easy to obtain a standard list of agents, but what's the story on each? Who are the

most ethical agents? Some authors with one or more bad experiences with agents hesitate to try any others. Or at least they become suspicious and are cautious about signing with another agent.

5. Some agents charge reading or consideration fees, which many authors resent.

6. Shocking as it may seem, some agents conveniently forget to send authors what is due them when it's time to settle up on royalties earned.

7. Using an agent for all contact with publishers prevents an author from gaining the experience of dealing with book editors directly.

Many editors in the business are courteous and reliable professionals with a keen interest in new books and ideas. An author can develop into a skilled salesperson through the experience of communicating with editors over a period of time.

In fact, some authors get so good at selling their books that they're advised on occasion to become agents themselves.

8. Some unscrupulous agents have been known to keep money collected from overseas sales. They just fail to report any of the sales to an author.

9. The author's work may be handled by a minor employee who has little or no experience and/or clout in dealing with publishers. This can happen with the larger agents.

10. A smart author can build his own list of good editors to contact. And if free to negotiate, such authors can communicate with new ·publishers coming into the business every month. In other words, an author can sell at his or her own pace and level instead of the agent's.

11. An author can choose to auction his or her book project to a number of selected publishers and then accept the best offer received. But an author's agent may not believe that an auction is appropriate for a particular book project.

In general, I advise you to seek out an agent no later than after signing your second book contract. Many pros in the publishing business feel that an author should seek an agent after the very first sale.

There's no guarantee that you'll get a good agent after three or even five book sales. Some of the leading agents already have more clients than they can properly handle. Some won't even reply to letters from new authors. Or they send form rejection replies. When they do consider taking on a new client, they may require that person to be a name author.

Get one best seller on your credit list, however, and most agents worth their salt will come after you like that speedy roadrunner of cartoon fame. A hot author naturally has a wider choice of agents.

A Four-Star Way to Get an Agent

One smart way to snag an agent to represent you is to sell a book project yourself. Then dangle the deal with the agent of your choice.

This method may work, because it offers tempting bait to the agent. In return for the agent's attention and acceptance of you as a client, you drop a book sale in the agent's lap and thus 10 percent of the advance and total royalties the resulting book earns.

Many agents find it hard to turn down such a sure thing. It's money in the bank for them.

Agents have been compared to antique dealers, because their competence varies greatly. This is a good reason to go slowly in deciding on an agent. Check out the ones you're considering. If at all possible, meet and talk with them personally.

Even if you never have an agent, don't let the lack of one keep you out of the book business. Many authors have built very successful, careers on their own without the services of an agent.

Mary Roberts Rinehart was once reported to be the highest paid author in America. An interesting fact about her was that she always worked without an agent.

If your books deserve to be published, there are editors waiting to read them. These editors will recognize the value of your books and act accordingly.

So remember. You can place your share of books all by yourself. But, as you make a name for yourself in the business, agents will be drawn to you like bees to honey.

CHAPTER TWELVE

Questions and Answers to Guide You

At one time or another in their lives, many people think that they might have at least one book in them. It's a bit sad that most never even make a start on a book. Who knows? A little encouragement might have helped them to get one or more books written.

Here are some frequently asked questions and answers about writing and selling books. They're meant to offer guidance and encouragement for your own writing:

How much money can I make writing books?

Anywhere from a few thousand dollars on up. The blockbuster books like *The Godfather, Jaws,* and *The Thorn Birds* pull in astronomical amounts. But quite a few books earn from $10,000 to $50,000 or more for their authors.

Which book publisher has had the most best sellers over the years?

At this writing, Doubleday is evidently still the leader. One source of this information—*70 Years of Best Sellers*—has Doubleday way out in front.

Could a person with just a love for books and reading be a possible future author?

Why not? The potential is certainly there. You'll start with a certain feeling, respect, and affection for books. I began this way. I enjoyed reading all kinds of books. I still do. And then one day I just said to myself: "Why don't I write a book?" And I did just that. I'm still at it today and expect to be for some time to come.

Isn't this the day of the non-book? I see many books in the stores that don't seem to be books at all but rather clever ideas or gimmicks put between covers to catch the public's fancy.

That's true. But bear in mind that the publishing business is growing larger every year. There's room in the book world for light and even frivolous books. A great many buyers of books seek entertainment. If a book amuses them, or makes them laugh or smile, they've gotten a plus from such a book. In fact, such books may be the highlight in a person's dull routine for that week or month.

How well do books written for teenage readers sell?

One teenage classic, *Going on Sixteen*, has sold well over 500,000 copies since 1946. This kind of book can obviously keep selling for many years.

I'd like to write a travel book. What advice can you give me?

Professional authors who specialize in travel books will often take a trip across their native country or some other one. They may take notes and conduct research along the way. After returning home, they write books based on their trips.

I did this myself a few summers ago. I took an extensive trip through the Midwest and western states. I took a lot of notes during my trip. When I got back home, I wrote an outline and sample chapter based on my travels. I haven't sold the project yet, but I believe I will eventually place it.

Alistair Cooke's best-selling book, *America,* was so popular and so well done that it resulted in a most successful television series under the same title. If done well, travel books can pay off for years. Cooke's excellent book was of course more an historical work, but it certainly stimulated the reader's interest in and love of travel.

Is it true that if one can write a book, he or she could also write a screenplay, a television script, a newspaper column, articles, or virtually anything?

It's generally true, but a lot depends on the particular author. Some are at home writing anything. Others prefer to specialize in one type of writing. A real writer, however, should be able to do almost any type of work, with a bit of study to learn the desired form and technique needed.

The late Rod Serling made a big name for himself mainly as a television writer. But he eventually realized some years before his death that he preferred to do books. As Rod put it at the time, "I will never work in TV again. It's too tough to be creative, to be unfettered in TV. TV was good to me, but I'm never going back. Oh, how I love the ease and freedom of writing books."

When an author sells a first novel or nonfiction book, is it better to stick with that same publisher on future books or play the field?

Many publishers used to include a clause in their contracts giving them an option on an author's next book. This clause is now usually omitted in most contracts.

So authors are not required to send their next books to the publishers of their earlier work. It's optional. They can if they wish.

But an author who was generally happy with a certain publisher may stick with the company for years. Other authors remain independent and place their books with a variety of publishers, often signing with the company that offers the best deal.

Doesn't it usually take some inside contacts to sell a book today?

An inside contact may give you a better chance to make a sale, but one of the most valuable tools for selling books is persistence.

In the words of Madden Cassidy, a British teacher, "Over the years, in my creative writing classes, I've noticed without exception that success comes not to the most talented people but to those, usually a shade less talented, who are really strong on persistence."

Should I compose a manuscript on the typewriter or write it out in longhand first?

You'll have to experiment to discover what works best for you. Some authors do all their work at their typewriters. Others feel the need to write in longhand first. In time, you'll discover the best way for you.

I prefer to write everything in longhand first. I then make corrections from that draft and type it up. If necessary, a second draft is then typed. Some books take many drafts and corrections. Others flow more smoothly.

Ernest Hemingway was reported to have rewritten the ending of *A Farewell to Arms* thirty-nine times. He did this on the manuscript itself and also the galley proofs.

What would you say is the most important element needed for writing a best seller?

Luck. The authors of the biggest selling paperback on Elvis Presley, *Elvis—What Happened?*, were already well into the book about the super rock star when Elvis suddenly died. So their book was one of the very first to hit the bookstores. The last report I saw on the book said it had sold over five million copies. By now, it's no doubt far beyond that figure.

Author N. Richard Nash had a novel published at the same time the cardinals in Rome joined together to choose a new pope. Nash's novel, *The Last Magic,* starts with a pope who is dying.

The timing of a book's publication can have a significant influence on its acceptance and success with the book buying public.

For a first novel, would I have a better chance of publication by writing a romance?

At this writing, romance books are still very much in demand. In fact, there seems to be a renewed interest in and appreciation of romance in general. It could last for several years or give way to another trend.

The Thorn Birds has no doubt had an influence. Many have called it the number one love story of recent years.

I think also that some women authors, going to bat on their first books, may have a better feel or instinct for writing a romance novel. There are of course several kinds of books that focus on romance. Some of these include the historical romance, sweet or savage romance, and even Gothics, which combine romance and suspense.

Do good or bad reviews help or hinder the sales of a book?

While good reviews may help to increase sales, negative ones don't usually determine the destiny of a book.

Don't most authors need a sympathetic editor?

Certainly many do. This is a major reason why many authors prefer to work with an editor who has also done some writing.

A number of articles I've read say that conglomerates have taken over and now run the book publishing industry. If so, then isn't this a bad time to try to be an author?

Conglomerates tend to focus on highly commercial books that offer the most promise of becoming big best sellers and returning a large profit on their investments. So other books, with possibly much more lasting value, may get lost in the shuffle. With so many new books being published each year, a growing number of other titles do risk being overlooked.

On the other hand, the reason that conglomerates have taken over in many cases is because they are attracted to money. They've watched the growing book publishing industry and decided that they wanted some of the action.

The book business is booming. Whatever you want to write, now is the time to do it. If one of your books doesn't click, another one may do so. You've got to keep the faith.

Can two or more books be written at the same time?

Some fortunate authors seem to do well with several books in progress at the same time. When they grow tired of working on one, or possibly hit a snag, they turn to the other books.

Other authors, however, cannot turn the writing process off and on so easily for different projects. They prefer to work on one book at a time. You'll have to experiment to find out the limits of your own powers.

There's an advantage to working on two or three book projects at the same time. It may keep you from getting stale.

Who owns the copyright on a book, the author or the publisher?

Most publishers are willing to take out the copyright in the author's name, if the author asks that it be done this way. Some contracts state that the copyright will be in the author's name. Others don't, so the author must request it.

A book contract is negotiable, so the author can ask for the changes that he or she wants. Most agents will attend to this automatically.

Aren't there too many books on the same subject, like Elvis Presley, for example?

This is true in a number of cases. People with very remote ties to Elvis (if any at all) have written books about him. And others who claim that "he spoke to me in a dream" (or in a seance) are also turning out books.

Elvis, I'm afraid, has been a commercial subject for obvious reasons. Plenty have jumped on the Presley bandwagon. More books are sure to be published about him. The trend may well continue through the rest of the century and longer since Elvis has become a strong cult figure like Bogart, Marilyn Monroe, Jean Harlow, Rudolph Valentino, and others.

The subjects that are currently hot naturally have competing books covering them. Jogging is a clear example. It's a very popular subject at this writing. People everywhere are obsessed with jogging. There must be a dozen new books on the subject, all competing with each other for the book buyer's money.

Should an author, whether a newcomer or veteran, write only what he or she knows?

This is an old bugaboo question that keeps popping up. Many authors would agree with you.

Personally, I believe that an author should feel free to write on any subject under the sun which is of interest. Some publishers lose out on good books, because they insist that certain subjects be tackled by experts only. Let's face it, most authors would run out of material quickly if writing only on subjects about which they already know a great deal.

I have a religious book idea. Should I contact a religious book publisher or query a general publisher who includes religion as a category on his list?

You can go either route. If your book will have appeal for both religious and secular markets, it might be best to try to interest a general publisher who does some religious titles each year. If your book can sell in both religious and general markets, you'll make far more sales.

Religious publishers have enjoyed a huge rise in their sales in recent years, and this trend should continue well into or possibly throughout the 1980s.

I must warn you, however, that a number of religious publishers fail to reply to letters and may hold your proposal or manuscript for an incredibly long period of time before reaching a decision. They report back to authors much more slowly than most general publishers. Some religious publishers also require a complete manuscript before they will make a decision.

It's usually a good idea to write a religious publisher first and ask them for some idea of how long a decision would take. Be sure to tell them whether you want to send a proposal, a partial manuscript, or a complete book.

See Chapter Twenty on writing religious-inspirational books. This chapter can save you a lot of time and effort. And it may help you sell your religious book much sooner.

What is the meaning of "subsidiary rights?"

Most think of it as the money paid for reprint rights to a book. The leading paperback publishers like Bantam, Fawcett Gold Medal and Crest, Pocket, Jove, Warner, and others often bid for the reprint rights to books that do well (or show early promise) in hardcover.

Subsidiary rights also cover radio, recording rights, book-club and micro-film editions, motion picture and television rights, syndication, the right to quote, mail-order, coupon advertising, and other rights.

Reprint, book-club, and second serial rights are usually divided equally (the money from such sales) between author and publisher.

Serialization rights are what newspapers and magazines buy, in order to print parts of books or condensations.

Should an author seek to work with a small, medium, or large publisher?

In a great many cases, the author has little choice. What often happens is that a publisher will respond to you, after your book project has been exposed to them and accepted.

With some success and credits back of you, however, you should have more clout going for you. You're certainly free to try to sell to publishers of your choice, whatever their size may be.

Generally speaking, some small publishers may be able to give your book more attention than a large company. But the larger publishers usually offer the biggest advances, which are important to a great many authors.

A good idea is to try all three kinds of publishers. Once you've had a book published by each, you'll know which size company you prefer to work with in the future. Many authors are unconcerned about the size of their publishers. They're just pleased to find a publisher for their books, regardless of the company's size.

Billy Graham has had a string of best sellers. How long does he take to write a book?

Graham has a big following. His instant recognition with the public, here and overseas, helps a lot. In his own words, he spends two months a year on his writing. "The books will be around long after I'm gone," he says.

How does the future look for paperbacks?

In a word, fantastic. Thousands of new retail outlets for paperbacks are opening up every year. As you know, many supermarkets, toy and card shops, and other general stores sell paperbacks. *Publishers Weekly* has had a number of reports on the growing importance of paperbacks. More paperbacks are definitely being used in the college classroom.

The demand for paperback originals is also increasing. Originals are often bought directly from the author. Many publishers are coming out with one or more paperback lines or buying controlling interest in such companies. Quality paperbacks, which are higher priced than mass market titles, are also growing in sales. Everything points to a continued boom for paperbacks in the years ahead.

So get busy and write some of your own. Then you'll be sure to get a slice of this paperback royalty pie. Some authors write paperbacks exclusively.

Won't the many publishing mergers of recent years mean a tougher time for unknown authors in the years ahead?

Yes, to a certain extent. *Publishers Weekly* reported some fifty-eight publishing company mergers the year before last. But I'm personally convinced that there will always be publishers, large and small, who will recognize the value of good books and publish them, whether the author is well-known or a complete newcomer.

I talked to some employees of a large mall bookstore I shop in frequently. They told me they were being crushed with the arrival of new books and have no room for them. Isn't this space problem getting worse in many store outlets?

Definitely. This is one of the key problems in the industry. As yet, nobody has really solved it. The focus is on publishing books that will move off the shelves and into the hands of customers.

The shelf life of new books can be very short. If a new book doesn't sell quickly, it gets returned to the publisher to make room for some other new arrivals.

It's much like two big tides. One tide of new books arrives in a store. At the same time, another tide of unsold books is moved out of the store and back to the publishers.

Just last week, I saw a young lady taking unsold books off the shelves in a large store. She smiled when she saw me watching her. I commented on the growing number of new books in her store. "Yes," she said. "These will have to go back to the publishers. They didn't sell. I feel sorry for the authors. They won't make any money on these."

Does an author have any control over the retail price of his or her book?

No. Most publishers (if not all of them) have the last word on a book's price. But some authors may express their opinions on the matter. And name authors may have some influence on the final price.

Do publishers get mad or irritated if a book is offered to them on auction? (The same book project is submitted to a number of publishers for the best offer.)

No. It's done a lot today. Publishers do feel, however, that the book being auctioned must be worthy, in other words, be a commercial and important project. And they expect the rules for any such auction to be spelled out; i.e., a deadline date for responding with an offer must be specified.

Must an advance against royalties be paid back by an author, if his or her book doesn't sell?

Some publishers used to include a clause in their contracts stating that unearned advances had to be paid back. Now an author is usually allowed to keep the advance. There are still some publishers around, however, who may expect the advance back, if the book doesn't sell enough copies to cover it.

Name the best-selling book of the last hundred years or so.

First published in 1868, *The World Almanac and Book of Facts* has sold over thirty-seven million copies.

CHAPTER THIRTEEN

Research and Interviews Add Depth

Whether you choose to write a novel or a nonfiction book, a must for your manuscript is research. It's a vital ingredient for producing a worthy book.

Books come to life with good research material. Enough thoughtful and imaginative research lets the reader know that the author has done his or her homework. The resulting book has substance and value.

The Benefits of Research

- You uncover important facts for your book.
- Your finished book is more significant and up-to-date.
- A greater demand for your book can be the result of important research. The new information you present may have a far-reaching influence on readers. It can affect their health, jobs, family life, stability, and general outlook.
- The research some authors do for historical novels can help put their books on the best-seller lists.

● The right kind of research aids an author in sensing what must be said in the book.

● Numerous authors have come across ideas and material for their next books while doing original research.

● Doing research for a book is fascinating for a number of authors. Some hate it. Others love it and thrive on it. A real danger can result in spending too much time on research so that it becomes an end in itself. Some authors fall into this trap.

● Research has power. It adds color, interest, reality, accuracy, believability, and the stuff of life itself to novels and nonfiction books.

How to Plan and Organize Your Research

Here are some helpful tips on doing research for the book or books I hope you're now planning to write. The list is by no means complete. If you're new to research, your librarian can help you a lot. Here are some useful pointers:

1. Begin with some background reading. If you're writing a novel, read about the period of time you plan to use; i.e., the Civil War, the Victorian period, or the eighteenth century. If your book is nonfiction, read for a general knowledge of the subject (books, encyclopedias, magazine and newspaper articles). Some books will be more useful to you than others. You can't read everything, so choose your selections carefully.

2. Some authors take notes while reading and record them on large or small index cards for later reference. Other authors like to use notebooks or large yellow legal tablets.

3. For novels, especially historical ones, you'll find it useful to make a list or sketch of the key events you want your characters involved in.

4. For nonfiction books, be sure to read other published

books on the subject, both old and new ones, along with articles in booklets, newspapers, and magazines.

5. When you know the place and time for your novel, you'll find that certain biographies and other books paint a good picture of the era. They can be a great help.

6. Government sources. Never overlook the government of your country as a possible source of material for your book. There may be agencies or branches of your government that can supply you with very useful information. You can ask for this material in person or write and request it. If your book is nonfiction and will have illustrations, you may be able to obtain some excellent photos from government sources.

7. Be alert for any diaries of the period you're writing about. Diaries have been written during any number of time periods. They can be useful for adding details about that day, including what people were thinking about, the popular songs or books of the time, and more.

I found the *Diary of Anne Frank* most inspiring and useful in capturing the feel of what it meant to live in hiding in Europe during World War II.

8. Don't forget various research institutes. Most countries have them. They might be able to provide you with some key information.

9. Old letters and documents may be good sources of facts for a variety of books.

10. Personal interviews remain one of the best ways to secure material for a book. I've done enough interviews for a dozen books. In other words, people themselves are an endless source of material.

Many are flattered by an author's request for an interview. Some people don't like to see an author use a tape recorder during the interview. So if you take notes, try to get down what they tell you as accurately as possible.

11. If possible, you may wish to visit the locale you are going to write about.

Make Your Research Time Count

While you're researching a book, use your time wisely. Get a jump on the day. Begin early. Get as much material and notes down as possible for each day.

Get to know some of the key people in the libraries you plan to use, for they can be of great help to you and save much of your time.

Remember that it doesn't take a genius to collect background material. Most people could do it with little or no trouble.

You want the time period used in your novel to be authentic. Your goal, certainly for historical novels, is to recreate the time during which your story unfolds.

Try also to determine well in advance how much time you plan to devote to the research stage of your book. Many authors work out a schedule for their research.

Planning the research stage in advance will also save you from backtracking. You'll know what to do each week, where to go for certain material, and how much more of it you need.

Personal Interviews Add Freshness

Some of the best material for your book can come from personal interviews. Keep this source in mind and try to line up the interviews you want in plenty of time, so that you'll have the notes from them ready when it's time to start writing your book.

An interview I was fortunate enough to obtain from a major Hollywood songwriter became the basis for one of the strongest chapters in my first published book, *How to Write Songs That Sell.*

I spent about four hours on two separate days in the home of this talented and very professional film songwriter and winner of three Academy Awards. I learned a lot about how he got started writing songs, his move to Hollywood, his growth through the years as a film writer, and his views on today's music and the songs of tomorrow.

It was the most fascinating interview I've conducted to date. And the material from the interview made a fine chapter on songwriting for motion pictures.

If you wish to interview some celebrity or entertainment name for your book, you may have to contact the person's public relations agent. From that point on, you may or may not be granted an interview, depending on the schedule of the person, your own previous track record, the nature of what you're writing, and other factors.

Some stars, celebrities, and key people you may want to interview can be contacted directly by mail. They may agree to an interview, depending on your letter, background, where the material will be used, and whether they can fit the interview into their work schedule.

The point is that you'll never know until you try to get an interview. Be sure to mention anything you've published in your letter—articles, books, or booklets. They're bound to help you get an interview.

The quotes you get in interviews add flavor and depth to your book. Many readers enjoy reading about the opinions of well-known or important officials, scientists, college professors, business executives, and radio, television, and film stars.

A good example of this interest in special people is the book currently very much in demand called *Mommie Dearest*. The book is about Joan Crawford's shocking treatment of her daughter. The book is receiving lots of attention. It will probably sell for some time to come.

Be Ready for Every Interview

Before you interview anyone—especially anyone well known or important—be sure you've done your homework. Read about the person, if he or she is a star, a celebrity, or famous in some way. Know the key facts about the person's life. This advance reading will help you during the interview and make it go more smoothly.

It's also very useful to have a list of questions you want to ask during ·each interview. This is a sound rule to follow, whether the person you interview is famous or not.

You can find the basic facts about well-known people in *Who's Who*. Many fields of endeavor have their own special directories and your librarian can help you find the ones you need to see.

Author John Brady has written a very helpful book called *The Craft of Interviewing*. It can guide you in all facets of interviewing.

Tape-Recorded Interviews

Some people, no matter who they are, don't like to be recorded. Before carrying a recorder with you for an interview, find out first if your subject has any objection to it. If so, you'll have to get along as best you can by taking notes throughout the interview.

After some experience at interviewing, you'll know what types of facts you can easily remember and those you need to get down on paper. Be especially accurate on all quotes, because in general people don't appreciate being misquoted.

Accuracy is important in recording all material. Statements people say can and are sometimes taken out of context. Learn to be a fair and accurate interviewer. You will be considered very professional if you are.

CHAPTER FOURTEEN

When It's Time to Start the Writing

I want to hit one point hard in the beginning and the end of this chapter: Bringing a new book to life is exciting.

Creating a book out of nothing is somewhat similar to childbirth. Whether it sells a million copies or only 5,000, there's something very satisfying, and even mystical, about bringing a new book into the world.

It's a "one on one" experience. It's your words and ideas which are being transmitted to the minds and hearts of readers you'll never meet personally.

But in the pages of your book, you do meet the reader. You, as the leader or storyteller, take him or her on a journey beginning on page one and ending at the last sentence.

Many authors think about this before starting a new book. They ask themselves some key questions such as the following: "How can I say what I want to say without boring the reader? How can I make the reader care about my characters and the situation they're involved in? How can I entertain or instruct the reader in this book?" These are important questions to ask before writing word one of your book.

Don't Let All That Material Scare You

Most authors never forget the experience of writing their first books. That first time at bat just stays more vivid in the mind's eye. And a lot of authors never lose their sense of pride or enthusiasm for their first books.

Whether the book you want to write is your very first or your fiftieth, don't let all the material you've gathered for your book scare you.

Some authors collect wheelbarrows of material for a book. When they're ready to start writing, they pile all the notes on their desk. Or they spread it out all over their office. Then they sit there for days just staring at that mountain of material.

You'll get yourself on edge, if you worry about how you're going to get that mountain of notes into the pages of a full-length book.

Here are some ways to view all the material you've gathered when you're ready to start writing:

• You don't have to use all of that mountain of notes. What you're after is the cream of the crop.

• If you already have an outline, you'll have a framework showing where the material will be used.

• You can soon make your mountain of notes much smaller by dividing it into the key parts of your book. This process will become clear to you by simply sorting through the material.

Get a handle on the beginning, middle, and ending of your book. Then the mountain of notes you first had in front of you has changed to three smaller stacks.

Break Your Material Down into Sections

One of the best ways to get organized for the actual writing of your book is to break down the mountain of notes and material you have into sections.

A number of authors like to use three by five cards for taking notes. When you've finished your research for a book, you can group the cards according to key sections. This basic method with variations seems to work for many authors.

You may use other methods to break down your material. You can use file folders or large envelopes to hold all the notes and material for major sections.

After you've divided the material into a number of sections, you'll usually find the task of writing looks easier. One reason for this is that you no longer have a huge mountain of material. You can see the various sections of your book and the material for each one.

Some authors simply file their notes and research information into three key sections—the beginning, middle, and end—and then go from there. Others like to use more sections. Again, you'll have to experiment to find out what methods you like best.

Chapters Will Fall into Place

If you don't already have an outline prepared for the chapters of your book, the various sections you place material in will often suggest chapter divisions.

In other words, your sections will become chapters. Whatever heading you use for a section may be a natural chapter heading or at least offer some hints for the title.

You can easily see now why having a list or outline of your book chapters is helpful. You then merely place the material you've obtained under each chapter.

Many authors use a file cabinet or desk drawer for the

material in their chapters. Others write the chapter title on a large envelope or folder and then place all the right notes and research materials inside that particular chapter.

This system allows you to line up the material for each chapter of your book. When you're ready to start writing, you simply pull out the material for that chapter and you're in business. You do the same for every chapter until you've completed your book.

There are other methods of organization, but this one is as good or better than most. You may find that you're the type of writer who just prefers to pile all your notes in one place and then start writing from there.

But a lot of authors like to break down the initial mountain of material into smaller, key sections. Remember, chapters make a book. It's comforting for an author to know that the material for each succeeding chapter is ready and waiting to be used. This system keeps you enthusiastic and helps you write.

Plan the Best Writing Schedule for You

If you hold down a regular nine to five job, it's obvious that the only time you can spend on your writing is either early in the morning or in the evening. You'll need some time for recreation and relaxation, so you'll have to try different schedules to find your best hours for writing.

Maybe you could get in two hours of writing in the morning before going to your job. Thousands of authors like the early hours when their minds are fresh. Or you could work from eight or nine at night to midnight.

Try to put in three hours a day at your writing, if at all possible. If there's no way you can do this, then settle for an hour in the morning or evening. Many books have been written by authors who had only an hour or less a day to devote to their writing.

It's important for some authors to write at the same

place and at the same time each day. The reason is that the mind becomes used to the routine and cooperates better than it would if you wrote at a different time and place each day. Other authors, however, can write no matter where they are or what time of day or night it is.

Some authors work hard Monday through Friday and then relax over the weekend. Others work the same hours at their writing desk seven days a week. There's a lot to be said for getting the first draft down on paper fairly quickly. This can be especially true when the book is a novel.

A long break from writing may cause difficulty in getting started again. There are natural rhythms in writing. And this is one reason why many authors like to work every day, when writing a book. A week or two away from your writing, or sometimes even a weekend, may interrupt your normal rhythm.

Writing Discipline Gets Results

Before you fall asleep at night, it helps to think about the next day's writing session. Your mind will often work out the best way to handle the next day's material.

The writing you do each day pays off in a number of ways. Some of them are:

● The next scene for your novel may fall into place in your mind the night before or you'll wake up knowing just how to handle it.

● The momentum you've established keeps you enthusiastic.

● It's been said that a real author is one who enjoys realizing how many new pages were completed for a given day or week. Writing discipline keeps the pages piling up.

● Writing discipline helps enormously in getting more books finished.

One has to admire an author like George Sand, who

stuck to her goal of thirty pages a night, no matter what.

There must have been any number of nights when George Sand didn't feel like writing, was upset about something, sad, lonely, or tired. But her goal was of prime importance to her. She absolutely refused to go to bed before writing her set number of pages.

George Sand, like John O'Hara, Steve Allen, and other authors, was basically a night writer. She preferred to write late at night.

Discipline can be vital to your growth and success as an author. Surprising though it may sound, there are authors who sign book contracts, receive and spend their advances, and then never complete the books.

Publishers have been burned by such authors. So they naturally look for assurances that an author—if not known to them—will actually finish a book.

When a contract is signed, an author may have every intention of completing the manuscript. But without enough discipline, it just may not work out that way. New authors must strive to develop discipline, for it can play a key role in leading them to success.

Most veteran authors know the importance of discipline in their work. They learn to get and keep discipline going for them. And it pays off in their being able to write books in greater quantity and of higher quality.

CHAPTER FIFTEEN

What about Length?

Length for a book was mentioned earlier, but you'll find more information on the subject useful.

To estimate the length of your manuscript, figure on about 250 words for each manuscript page. If a manuscript you complete runs 200 pages, that means the total number of words is about 50,000.

Though you may arrive at 200 pages for a given manuscript, the published book may run somewhat less than that. The length you get may not be the same as for the final product, but the difference is usually slight, unless of course there are photographs or other illustrations.

Some Novels Dictate Their Own Length

It's usually a mistake to predict the length of a novel you plan to write. It may run much longer or shorter than you originally intended.

Novels run from about 100 pages to over 1,000. Family-saga type novels usually run considerably longer than a general novel. You'll find the following table on various novel lengths helpful:

Fiction

GENERAL NOVELS—100 to 300 pages. Many run close to 200 pages.
FAMILY SAGAS—500 to 1,000 pages (or more).
ROMANCES—300 to 700 pages. They can run more or less.
ADVENTURE NOVELS—200 pages or more on the average.
MYSTERY NOVELS—About 200 pages or thereabouts.
HUMOROUS AND MISCELLANEOUS NOVELS—100 to 200 pages.

Nonfiction

Nonfiction books run from 100 pages or so up to 1,000 pages and more. Many of them are in the neighborhood of 200 to 300 pages. *American Caesar,* the book on MacArthur by William Manchester, has 709 pages. Richard Nixon's memoirs runs 1,090 pages.

Full Value for Their Money

The length of a book can have an influence on a decision to buy or not. I've often watched browsers in bookstores examine the thickness of a book, either before or after noting the price.

People in general do tend to feel that a $10 or $12 book should offer a suitable thickness. I think book buyers in general forget that it's not how many pages in a book that matter most but what's on those pages.

A name author may get away with a shorter book. The name recognition makes up for the price. But the average book buyer thinks seriously before spending $12.50 or $15 for a book.

Many business and professional type books are priced over $20. So the size of these books are usually carefully noted in relation to the asking price.

Buyers tend to feel that they're getting their money's worth if the book they're considering is thick in relationship to the price printed on the inside flap.

Short Books Are Best Sellers Too

Don't think that a book has to be 1,000 pages or more to become a best seller. Short books have also done well. They will most probably continue to do well in the years ahead. Not all of them sell big of course, but some of them catch on every year and chalk up very respectable showings.

A number of book buyers evidently make their decisions to purchase a book on pure impulse. So if a given book strikes a browser's fancy, he or she may buy, whether it's a short or long book.

Acres of Diamonds is a short book, but it has sold well for many years. So have the following other short books:

You Were Born on a Rotten Day
How to Speak Southern
Return From Tomorrow
How to Advertise

Length Usually Takes Care of Itself

The average length of most books is about 200 pages more or less. But this doesn't mean that a book of yours can't run 125 pages, 250, or over 500.

Each book tends to forge its own length. Just write until the story you're telling reaches a conclusion or your nonfiction book comes to a satisfying and logical ending.

Some Publishers Have Minimum Lengths

When you have a publisher in mind for one of your book projects, it's wise to check out their length requirements. You can find them in the market books for authors which are published annually.

Many of the listings state a minimum length of 50,000 to 60,000 words. One major publisher in the East wants nothing under 80,000 words.

Many book publishers are flexible, however, and may be willing to accept a shorter or longer length than what is stated in the market information for their company.

Remember this key point about length: It's usually much easier to cut the length of a manuscript than to add more to it at the last minute. This is especially true after a manuscript has been delivered to a publisher and the process leading to publication has begun.

Religious Publishers Take Shorter Books

A number of religious book publishers will take on books of shorter length. I've seen many such books in recent years, and the length has often run at about 20,000 or 30,000 words. Many others have a total length of 35,000 to 40,000 words. A religious or inspirational book can be only 100 or 125 pages and still sell many copies. Some seem to make their way in the book world, regardless of their brevity.

Write Books with Various Lengths

If you plan to write more than one book in the future, a good general rule is to not limit yourself to any certain length. Shoot for a variety of lengths.

Your first book might run about 150 pages. Your second one could be shorter or longer at 200 to 300 pages.

In the course of your writing, you'll probably do both

long and short books and any number of books closer to the standard length of 200 or so pages.

Just let each book lead the way. It's what you say on those pages that's important. So don't worry about the length. Say what you need to say. Then stop.

CHAPTER SIXTEEN

How Many Drafts Does It Take?

The answer to the key question of how many drafts it takes for a well-written book depends on the author and the nature of the work.

The majority of authors accept the truth that most books require some degree of revision. There just aren't too many authors who can sit down and turn out hundreds of pages of perfect prose. Rewriting is part of an author's trade.

Rosemary Rogers, the prolific author of historical novels, rewrote *Sweet Savage Love* twenty-three times before sending it to Avon Publishers in New York. Her book became a big best seller and has sold 2.7 million copies to date.

The point is that revision can and does improve a manuscript. Few authors have the patience to rewrite one twenty-three times, but many who earn their living by the pen believe in at least several revisions.

Ways to Revise Your Work

There are several methods of rewriting your manuscript. You'll want to try each one, so you can discover which you prefer. These revision choices include the following:

1. Do one or more complete rewrites of your manuscript.

2. Change and correct your manuscript as you go along. In other words, make corrections on each page as you write it.

3. After completing a first draft, go back over the complete manuscript, writing in all changes and corrections with a red pencil or pen. Then type a fresh copy.

4. Write one or more chapters and then revise them before proceeding further with your book.

5. Rewrite the work as many times as you feel are necessary to get it the way you want it.

Some Books Turn Out Well with Slight Revision

Some authors do too much revision. They seem obsessed with reworking a manuscript and are never satisfied.

There comes a point with every manuscript when it's time to let go of it and to send it on its way to market. Part of the reason some authors can't let a manuscript go is a fear that it won't sell or that it can still be improved.

Authors can get so close to a manuscript that it's like parting with a baby; they hate to say good-bye. Quite a few feel let down when they reach the end of a book.

When you've done your level best on a manuscript and honestly believe that you can't improve it anymore, send it to a publisher. Then try to forget it. Turn to a new project. Better still, relax for a week. You've earned a break.

Too much revision can ruin some books. And it's also true that books you may write in the future will call for less rewriting than others.

If your strength lies in the novel, for example, you may need less revision in your fiction writing than on a nonfiction book. The reverse may also be true. Some authors will need to do more rewriting on novels and less on nonfiction.

In time, you'll be able to trust your own instincts. Something will tell you that a manuscript you've completed needs a rewrite or that it should have two more drafts. At other times, you'll be certain that a book you've completed needs only some minor corrections.

Best Sellers Take Revision

I can't guarantee that you'll have a best seller, just because you rewrite the work three or more times. But the history of best sellers indicate that a lot of them had a considerable amount of revision done on them.

A piece of writing can definitely be improved through revision. And such effort can and does pay off for an author in terms of a better selling book and quite possibly a best seller.

Ways to Revise and Improve Your Book

Here is a list of some of the ways a book manuscript may be strengthened:

- Change long and confusing sentences to short and clear ones. This can help just about any manuscript.
- Cut out technical words. Replace them with simple ones.
- Make paragraph transitions smoother.
- Shorten paragraphs that are too long. Break them up into shorter and medium length ones.
- Cut material in a novel that doesn't seem to move the story along (sections that go off in other directions).
- Rewrite material that is wordy.

- Dialogue is important in a novel, but avoid too much of it; otherwise the entire book becomes all dialogue. Alternate the flow of dialogue with narrative and descriptive passages.
- Edit out material that is repetitious. Don't repeat what you've already said unless you wish to emphasize a point.
- Get variety in your nonfiction books. Don't present the material in the same old way.
- Check to see there are plenty of examples and anecdotes in your nonfiction books. More can usually be added.
- Limit the use of dots and dashes.
- Rewrite sections that just don't ring true.
- Correct grammatical errors, spelling, and punctuation.

As long as you write, you'll profit from revision. Practically all books can benefit from some degree of revision.

Best-selling author Irving Wallace says it this way: "Even the most prestigious writers still sit by themselves, alone—applying the seat of the pants to a chair—and with their tortured psyches and numbed fingers write and labor. That's the name of the game—work, patience, and revision.

CHAPTER SEVENTEEN

Children's Books Can Sell for Years

With some writing experience and knowledge behind you, one day you might think about doing a children's book. I advise you not to begin your writing in this field. Books for children are special. You need a keen understanding of the children of this generation.

Advances for a children's book run $1,000 and up. How much you can get depends on your previous track record.

At the present writing, new mass market books for children are much in demand. Three of the most popular and successful children's book authors spoke at the last annual meeting of the American Booksellers Convention. About 1,600 people listened to Judy Blume, Theodor Geisel (Dr. Seuss), and Maurice Sendak talk about their new books and the exciting field of children's books.

How to Get Started Writing for Children

Most of those who think about writing a book for children wonder how they can get started. Judy Blume tried at first to follow in the steps of authors she admired. "Realizing I would never be another Dr. Seuss or Maurice Sendak, I turned to novels and wrote the kind of books I wanted to read when I was a kid."

An understanding of today's children is vital for success with this type of book. Children don't like to be talked down to, and they're not often fooled. The more you know about the children of today, the better your chances will be to write a successful book.

When you feel ready to try a project, query a likely publisher with a description of your idea or an outline and a chapter or two. Some publishers require a complete manuscript.

If you're in doubt as to which publishers to try, look over the special announcement issues on new children's books. These issues are published by *Publishers Weekly* in the fall and spring. In this way, you can study all the new children's book titles and see which publishers might be right for your book.

Some publishers break down their juvenile and children's book needs into the following divisions:

Picture books—for children ages three to eight or four through seven.

Fiction and Nonfiction—for ages eight through twelve.

Special interest books for young to older teens—eleven through eighteen.

Humorous novels and science fiction for ages nine through twelve.

Middle readers are usually thought to be those from ages seven to twelve. Young adults are eleven and up.

Readers from ages eight to twelve often enjoy books about far away places and various products in use.

The young teen group likes books on careers, hobbies, the family, government, outer space, and other subjects.

The older teen group is much into special interest areas like military service, art, music, and theater.

Here are some examples:

The Enormous Crocodile (good for ages three and up)
How to Enjoy Life Between 12 and 20 (teen appeal)
The Boy With the Special Face
Daredevils of the Speedway
Growing Up in the Age of Chivalry

Children will read about anything. But as a general rule, the following topics are always popular:

1. Humor
2. Fantasy
3. Mystery
4. Romance
5. Historical settings
6. Westerns
7. School problems
8. Books with heroic characters

It's always a help to go over some of the best-selling children's books already published. Here are some representative titles with the names of the publishers. All were best sellers:

Bear Party (Viking)
Between Planets (Scribner's)
The Call of the Wild (Macmillan)
The Christ Child (Doubleday)
The Cat in the Hat (Random House)

Careers Outdoors (Thomas Nelson)
How Big Is Big? (Addison-Wesley)
Little Lord Fauntleroy (Dutton)
America and Its Presidents (Grossett and Dunlap)

Children's Book Week

A most popular event in the United States is the annual Children's Book Week. New books that show promise and favorite titles from the past are highlighted at this time. Libraries, school book fairs, and retail stores work together to make the event a success.

Since many adults buy books for children, this special week is very helpful. Some big sellers in the Memphis and Mid-south area during last year's special week for children's books included the following titles:

The Little Prince—for ages four to ten
The Nutshell Library—a group of titles for ages three to
   six
The Chronicle of Narnia—for age nine and up
A Very Young Dancer—a photo-book popular with
   children

If this field of children's books holds an interest for you, you should check to see if such a special kind of week is observed in your area. Attend some of the programs and spotlight the books that are popular with children and adults who buy them. You can get ideas for new children's books in this way.

An outline for a children's book might run just a few pages or up to ten pages or more. Try to make your outline clear as to what each chapter in your book would cover. And give the chapter headings if at all possible.

A book by Dr. Seuss—*The Cat in the Hat*—has sold constantly. I suggest that you look the book over carefully.

The publisher is Random House. Dr. Seuss is credited with originating the picture book form.

A key point to remember is that a paragraph in a children's picture book is equal to a chapter in a book for adults.

Judy Blume

Author Judy Blume has been highly praised for making reading an exciting activity for children. One of her books, *Are You There God—It's Me, Margaret,* is the story of a child's life.

Judy was once a teacher at New York University. She went through two years of rejections before she began to sell her books. She wrote from the child she was.

In a ten-year period, Judy wrote seven books. Today she receives some 12,000 letters a year about her books. Her specialty is writing about the secrets of children and their problems.

Judy has an adult novel out and believes strongly that "writers need a chance to explore new directions." She has proved that she can write books in other areas. She's not limited to doing children's books.

Maurice Sendak, who has written dozens of books for children, has a strong hope that the children's book will not be isolated from other literature.

Children's books can keep selling for years. This fact may motivate you to sooner or later try your own hand at writing a book for children. Some juveniles sell for twenty years and longer. And each new crop of children means more potential buyers. As Maurice Sendak puts it, "We stay in print for decades."

Maybe you'll find a happy and successful place for yourself in this field of children's books. If so, you'll be helping to shape the men and women of tomorrow. Children are special. And that goes double for the books written for them.

CHAPTER EIGHTEEN

Writing the How-to Book

The how-to book has really come into its own in recent years. People everywhere seem to be more aware of the passing of time. So they want to get more out of their short journey through life.

How-to books have a wide appeal and often become strong sellers. Many of them become backlist titles and go on selling for years.

How-to books cover just about all areas of life today. Just name a subject. Chances are good there's a how-to book on it. A fantastic number of how-to books are available today in many countries.

One New York bookseller, Barnes and Noble, has estimated that how-to books account for about 30 percent of trade book sales.

My first published book was a how-to. I had been a published and recorded songwriter for years. I had a strong knowledge about writing and selling songs. So one day I just started a book on the subject. I called it *How to Write Songs That Sell.*

I learned even more about songwriting in the process of writing the book. And I got a great sense of satisfaction from doing the book. If you're very interested in a subject, you're naturally going to do a better book on it. And I've always loved the art and craft of songwriting for fun and profit.

Some Things You Need to Know about the How-to Book

● Stay aware of the variety of subjects you can write how-to books about.

● You may have to settle for a low advance on your first how-to book (perhaps $1,000 or $2,000). You can usually get larger advances on succeeding books.

● If at all possible, locate and talk to authorities on the subject of your book. Put what they tell you into your manuscript, and it will add weight to the book.

● The readers of this kind of book want to know how something is done. Tell them in a clear, simple, and interesting way.

● Query publishers first with a description of the project. And you'd be smart to see if the publisher you have in mind has any how-to titles on his list. Some publishers don't do this type of book or have a lesser degree of interest in it.

● The subjects that interest you personally may make good how-to books. What do you know best? What are some of your strong interests? What can you do well? Special hobbies of yours might result in an idea. These questions offer clues for possible how-to books.

● The more knowledge of or experience with a given subject you have, the more convinced an editor will be that you could do a good job on the book. So emphasize your skill or background on the subject. Publishers are looking for authors with the credentials to write how-to books on a variety of subjects.

● Both paperback and hardcover publishers use how-to books.

● Your enthusiasm for a how-to subject is often the first step in doing a book on it.

● Some publishers will take a new book on the same how-to subject. In other words, they may already have a how-to on a certain subject, but they may be interested in a new book. Some publishers like to have several books on the same subject.

● When you prepare a sample chapter or two for your how-to book, be sure to be specific enough. Your sample material must help sell an editor on your book.

Examples of How-to Books

Here are some examples of how-to books. Notice the variety of subjects:

How to Flatten Your Stomach
How to Read a Wine Label
How to Be Your Dog's Best Friend
How to Enjoy Ballet
How to Meet Men Now That You're Liberated
How to Improve Your Health
Priceless Gifts (How to Give the Best to Those You Love)
*Eurail Guide—How to Travel Europe and All the World
    by Train*
How to Get the Most Out of Your Cruise to Alaska
How to Laugh at Meat Prices

Some of the above how-to titles show that you can sometimes get away with a long title for this kind of book.

Ideas for How-to Books

From my own experience, I can vouch for the fact that ideas for new how-to books can come in a flash. Or they can come to you after a lot of thinking about new book projects you might like to do.

Such how-to ideas may occur to you at any time or place. So be ready. Ideas for this type of book may come from your own reading, experiences, and understanding of the needs, desires, and interests of people in general.

Here are some typical traits of an effective how-to book idea:

1. It's an attractive, catchy, and/or up-to-date idea.
2. The resulting book would have definite value for the reader.
3. The project is worthy of being published now.
4. You're capable of completing the book and are enthusiastic about it.
5. The idea has staying power. The finished book would have continuous appeal to help keep it selling for years.
6. It's an idea that may reflect an interest, trend, or happening a year from now.

There were few how-to books around in the 1960s. Their appeal was only slight a few years ago. Within the last couple of years, the demand for this book category has increased markedly until it now commands about 30 percent of the trade book market.

One author, who specializes in this how-to category, wrote four different how-to books in eighteen months. He also had three more similar books under contract and three others being edited. Not bad at all. It's true, however, that some authors have a natural feel and ability for this type of book.

Think Well about Writing a How-to Book

This kind of book offers you an excellent chance to sell

your first book and see it in published form, either paper-back or hardcover.

Believe me, your enthusiasm in selling your first book could easily draw you into writing on a part-time basis and maybe later even full-time.

So think well about creating a how-to-do-it book. It's a good way to start writing. Read how-to books yourself. And try to pick a subject that you know well and could explain with clarity and enthusiasm.

You'll be well paid in most cases for writing a how-to book. You can usually get a larger advance for additional books you write in this field. The how-to book is also a good bet if you're a veteran author with plenty of experience.

By selling your project first, using an outline or sample material, you can proceed with the rest of the book, knowing that it has a home when finished. That helps a lot.

I kid you not when I say that the how-to book can be your entrance into the fascinating book business. And if you already know your way around in the industry as an experienced or proven professional, the how-to book can add lots of green stuff to your bank account.

So read and write new how-to books for fun and profit. They can help establish you as an author.

CHAPTER NINETEEN

Hooked on Historical Romances

There are two basic ways to get hooked on historical romances. One way is to read them. The other is writing them.

As you might expect, women book buyers are the greatest fans of the historical romance. But lots of men read these popular books too.

Women authors sometimes do amazingly well on their very first historical romance. There's a strong attraction for a woman who wants to write to try her hand at this type of book.

Women who buy historical romances like plenty of action, romance, and generous amounts of sex. The magic ingredients of love and romance are what millions of women readers cannot resist. If the new historical romance novels they see in the bookstores seem to have these ingredients, many women will buy the books.

Dr. Joyce Brothers feels that love is the miracle drug of life. She defines love as "having the same care and concern for someone else as you would have for yourself. Most people are not aware that you can make love last a lifetime."

Part of the reason for the success of historical romances is the desire for love and romance. A great many women all over the world never get enough of either in their lives.

These books transport women readers into a world of exciting romance, passion, and suspense. They forget their own troubles for a while. They share, if only temporarily, the on-going experiences with the main character of the book. They're in on the romance, sex, and love of the heroine.

Dr. Carol Vandiveer, a psychiatrist and assistant professor at the University of Tennessee Center for the Health Sciences, recently stated that "it's been noticed for a long time that more diagnosed depressives are women. This is an accepted truth in all different countries."

So there's no doubt that reading historical romances can offer release and escape for millions of women. It helps them to enter a historical setting—a fictional character's world—and to follow the character as she copes with her own set of problems, goals, and experiences.

So women readers identify with the character's fulfillment and thus share in it vicariously.

There are strong reasons for believing that the historical romance will continue to sell in the years to come. If you're a potential woman author, you should give some serious thought to writing this kind of book. You might do very well indeed on your first time at bat.

If you enjoy reading historical romances, so much the better. You already know the basic form for such books. If you haven't read too much in the field, read several books as you think about writing one of your own.

Barbara Ferry Johnson

Barbara Johnson, author of *Tara's Song*, believes that

some paperbacks are beginning to be thought of as good literature. "Women still buy magazines with little novels in them, but since the emergence of the affordable, varied paperback, they're turning more to them."

Mrs. Johnson teaches English at Columbia, South Carolina College. She does careful research for each of her books. "The historical part is most vital to me. My books aren't Gothic romances; the difference is that they're more historical. There are love scenes, but I'm not clinically descriptive. And my heroines are not promiscuous. There's a difference between rape and seduction."

Lionors was Mrs. Johnson's first novel, an historical romance about King Arthur and a mysterious mistress by the name of Lionors.

Delta Blood was Mrs. Johnson's second novel. Set during the Civil War period in New Orleans, the book stayed on the *New York Times* best-seller list for eleven weeks.

Tips on Getting Ideas for Historical Romances

● Cities and countries can be rich in ideas. Soak up some of the history of a particular city or country you'd like to write about. Travel can yield a bonanza of ideas.

● Historical societies, meetings, and associations may lead you to worthwhile ideas.

● Old legends may suggest wonderful historical romance ideas.

● Play the game of what if. What if a certain character found herself caught up in a sequence of events? Experiment both on paper and in your mind. Turn ideas over regularly and consistently.

● Items you read about anywhere can be a springboard to a book idea in this field.

● Read published historical romances. They may suggest a locale, heroine, or historical era to you for a book you can write and sell.

• Your own memory may touch off a good book idea.

• Historical battlefields may suggest a book idea to you. Shiloh, Vicksburg, and Gettysburg have all suggested ideas to authors. The same is true for battlefield landmarks in England, France, Canada, Scotland, Australia, and other countries.

• The art of listening itself, conventions you attend, the conversations and remarks of others, their experiences, newspaper features and columns, and just living in general can all produce workable ideas for new historical romances.

Writing an Historical Romance

1. Realize from the start that readers of this kind of book want escape. Make sure you get it into your book.

2. Your main character will often emerge from the era or background you've chosen to write about. Live the life of your heroine in your mind. Identify with her as the story progresses.

3. Make sure you have a strong theme for your book before you begin. If you can express the theme in one simple sentence, so much the better.

4. Develop a difficult situation for your heroine to face.

5. The man in your heroine's life is a source of strength. He helps her to cope with a trying situation.

6. Pick a day to make a start on your book, whether it's research you do, planning and writing an outline, or completing the first page of the actual book.

7. Set yourself a goal of so many pages a week or month or so many chapters over a period of time. Then work toward that goal.

8. Once you have about fifty pages and an outline, you can try to interest an agent. Or you can try to sell your project directly to a publisher. Be sure to write first for their okay to send your material, for that's always better

than just mailing it in cold. If they're expecting it, they're more likely to give it some attention and get back to you sooner about it.

9. Strive to make the dialogue in your historical romance ring true. Does it sound right for the characters?

10. Rewrite those parts of your manuscript that need it. Most writing can usually be improved.

11. Don't give up if one, two, or a dozen publishers reject your book. The next publisher you try might accept it. Keep trying.

Don't automatically believe that you can't write an historical romance, if you hold down a regular nine to five job. One author, John Erskine, wrote his first best seller by working just two hours a night for five months in 1925. The finished book was *The Private Life of Helen of Troy*. During the day, he handled a full university schedule.

The Formula for Successful Historical Romances

Try to write the kind of book you'd enjoy reading yourself—for escape, relaxation, and sheer entertainment.

Spend some time on your book. The big selling historical romances aren't churned out in a week or so. Some authors spend a year or so just in the research stage. "Research is a compulsion with me," admits Rosemary Rogers.

Work to get suspense, intrigue, and action in your book. Make the reader unable to put the book down. Keep him or her eager to get into the next chapter.

After you've written one or more books in this field, you can begin to think about specializing in historical romances. This type of book has been good to many authors, mostly women.

Some women have become rich writing historical romances. You might do the same and one day join their elite group.

In the words of Paul Reynolds, a top New York literary agent, "It's better to discover your forte, concentrate on it so as to be typed. This is the type of author headed for the big time."

In other words, as Reynolds puts it, "A successful writer is known for a certain kind of story or type of writing."

If the historical romance is your kind of book, I hope you build a solid reputation in this field. And may your first historical romance be a best seller. That's the best kind to write. But every book of this type that you write and sell to a publisher is a real achievement. And you'll know it when you see your book in print.

CHAPTER TWENTY

Try Your Pen on a Religious-Inspirational

The last several years have seen a remarkable rise in the popularity of religious-inspirational books. At this writing, the end is nowhere in sight. Religious books have become very big business.

Part of the reason behind this boom in religious books is a new movement on the campuses of many colleges. This new movement highlights the basic theme that "God is alive." It's just the opposite from the movement of the 1960s, which held that "God was dead."

Religious class enrollment in colleges is way up. Many courses are crammed with students, and they're asking a lot more questions. The "God is dead" view has come full circle to "God is very much alive, well, and active."

Interest in religion seems to run in cycles. The current widespread popularity of religious and inspirational books may last for some time to come or just run its course in a few more years. It may die down somewhat through the 1980s and then pick up new momentum in the 1990s, building to a climax as the century nears its end in the year 1999.

There's a good chance that religious books will sell well for the rest of the century. Many people believe that the world is moving toward some climactic and momentous event in the year 1999 or 2000.

The point is that the time is very ripe for all kinds of religious and inspirational books.

There may be one or more such books ahead for you, if you choose this category.

The Evangelical Book Boom

Since the early 1970s, the growth rate per year in evangelical book sales has been a remarkable 18.9 percent according to a report by the Association of American Publishers.

Evangelical book sales reflect the strength of the evangelical movement of recent years.

The theme of the evangelical movement is the "born again" philosophy.

According to the Christian Booksellers Association, the total sales of "born again" religious publications reached $600 million last year.

Christian tee-shirts alone will add up to $5 million for this year.

Christian broadcasting organizations also spent more money last year to communicate their message on radio, film, and television. The Billy Graham Association spent $8.8 million on broadcasting media. The Christian Broadcasting Network spent $20 million to broadcast on more than 130 television stations.

All of these expenditures prove that religion is big business. Furthermore, it's growing larger every year. And a major part of it is the sale of religious books. This is all the more reason for you to write one or more religious books.

The Evangelical Book Defined

- Many think of the evangelical book as Bible centered.
- An evangelical book can have an affect on the world.
- The evangelical book dwells on the fact that "Christ died for our sins." Books such as this see the death and resurrection of Jesus as a central fact of life.
- The scriptures are taken seriously.
- Little faith is given to the here and now. The faith of the evangelical is in the redeeming work of Christ.

Some examples of evangelical books include *Doorways to Discipleship, What Does It Mean to Be Born Again, A Transformed Mind and Heart, God Can Make It Happen,* and *God Forgives Sinners.*

Karl Barth, the noted theologian, defined evangelical as being "informed by the gospel of Jesus Christ by a direct return to the Holy Scripture."

So think of the evangelical book as having a sense of mission. This type of book meets a need and is meant to touch lives in a deeper way than secular books.

General Religious and Inspirational Books

Numerous other books fall within the religious or inspirational category. They may not be purely evangelical, as many define it, but they're still books that uplift the human spirit, provide light along life's way, and point to the eternal values of love, beauty, hope, and faith.

Such books are often based on a personal experience of the author or give insight into various ways of coping with life's problems. Here are some examples:

In His Strength (Regal Books)
Beyond Death's Door (Thomas Nelson)

Marriage in Today's World (Herald Press)
Good News Is for Sharing (David C. Cook Publishing Company)
This We Believe (Bethany Press)
The Christian's Secret of a Happy Life (Revell)

There are times when religious books will far outsell the widely reported best sellers. Those who compile various best-seller lists don't generally check with religious bookstores. This is a major reason why a number of top selling religious books don't show up on such lists.

The Importance of the Religious Market

Evidence continues to grow that secular publishers are realizing the importance of the religious market more and more. More secular publishers were present for last year's Christian Booksellers convention than ever before.

An increasing number of Christian bookstores are being opened in major shopping districts and malls. Many of these stores used to operate in low-rent areas or from various side streets.

According to a key officer of the Christian Booksellers Association, the sales from Christian books now add up to over $600 million a year. At least one new Christian bookstore is opened every day.

A study conducted by Knowledge Industry Publications cites a trend that is having a favorable influence on religious book sales, namely, the aging of the population. Those in the twenty-five to forty-four-year-old age bracket are big buyers of religious books. The number of those in this age bracket is expected to increase by some 11 million in the next four or five years.

In the last five years, more than thirty religious books have sold over a million copies. One book alone, *The Living Bible*, sold over 18 million copies in the same time period. In the words of a Doubleday editor, one of the fastest selling books that publisher has ever had was *Angels: God's Secret Agents* by Billy Graham.

All of this should convince you that the future for religious-inspirational books is a very bright and successful one. Now is the time to write such a book of your own or several of them.

How to Write and Sell the Religious-Inspirational

1. Query a likely religious publisher, after requesting the catalogs of a number of companies and studying their lists.

2. Briefly describe the book you have in mind, explaining why you believe it would be a worthy addition to their line and what competing books there are on the subject (this is optional). Include a working title for your project if possible. You should also ask if you may send an outline and one or two sample chapters.

3. If you get a green light to send your project, mail your outline, chapters, and/or partial manuscript to the editor who has expressed interest in your book.

4. Then be patient. As a rule, religious publishers take longer to reach a decision than a number of secular companies. Some, however, are more prompt than secular publishers. You should be prepared to wait for six weeks to several months. An agent can get you faster decisions.

5. When you first contact a publisher, it's helpful to ask how long they take to report back on material sent. If you don't wish to wait up to several months, you can try some other publishers. It naturally takes longer for an editor to respond to a manuscript or partial one than to get back to you regarding an outline and chapter or two.

6. Remember, some religious publishers require a complete manuscript before they'll consider publishing your book.

If and when you send a complete manuscript, you may

be in for a very long wait before you get a final decision. Unless you have the time to write a full manuscript (not knowing if you can place it or not) and wait several more months to get a decision on it, I advise you to deal only with those religious publishers who are willing to reach a decision based on an outline and a chapter or two.

7. Consider this idea: If your religious-inspirational book project would be a title that could cross borders and sell in both secular and religious markets, you might try to place the book with a general publisher that includes religious-inspirational titles in its line.

More and more, religious publishers are selling their books in Christian bookstores and general bookstores as well. General publishers are doing the same thing, trying to get more of their suitable books into Christian bookstores. The point is that your book will sell more copies, if it can be on the shelves of both religious and general bookstores.

A Warning Worth Remembering

I don't know why it is, but some religious book publishers just aren't as professional, courteous, and businesslike as many general publishers are.

Maybe it's because they're smaller companies. Being in the business of publishing religious books, you'd think that they would be highly professional, courteous, and prompt in their dealings with authors. Most are. But you may encounter an occasional unprofessional company.

Most religious publishers will probably treat you honestly and fairly. And most will report back to you within a month to six weeks. But there are some incompetent editors in religious publishing, just as there are in general books. So be ready to pull out fast, if and when you run into bad apples.

Some religious publishers don't offer an advance against

royalties to an author. So if you do business with such a company, you must realize that it may be some time before the book is published and on sale. Some publishers can get a book on the market in six months. Others take a year or even longer.

The Rewards of Writing Religious-Inspirational Books

Despite some of the disadvantages of writing this kind of book, there are definite rewards to be gained. The advantages include the following:

- The satisfaction of knowing that your book may help someone at a crucial period in his or her life.
- The great variety of inspirational and religious subjects that you may choose to write about.
- The joy of seeing your book sell in both Christian and secular (general) bookstores.
- A chance to share your personal experiences with readers and to tell what your faith has meant to you.
- The opportunity to lead others closer to God.
- The satisfaction of knowing that your book may be around for many years to come and may make the world a better place in which to live.

CHAPTER TWENTY-ONE

The Market for Business and Professional Books

The 78 percent increase in sales for professional books over the last seven years is strong proof that this kind of book is well worth your time and effort. The source for these figures is the Association of American Publishers.

Professional book sales were up by 12 percent for last year. Publishers of this type of book are optimistic for the years ahead. Active promotion has not yet been focused on this area of the industry.

A key point you'll want to remember about this kind of book is the fact that a business or professional book can go on selling for many years. Here are some examples of business and professional books:

The Business Executive's Handbook
Creative Selling Through Trade Shows
The Ambitious Woman's Guide to a Successful Career
Winning at the Game of Success
The New Money Dynamics

How to Sell a Business or Professional Book

A good way to make a sale in this book category is to sit down and list the businesses or industries you've had experience in over the years.

Perhaps you have some special knowledge or information about advertising, insurance, safety and security, banking, transportation, music, government, real estate, lumber, beauty secrets, health care, teaching, or any number of other subjects.

It's entirely possible that you already have enough knowledge of a particular business or profession to make at least a good start on a book. Search your own background and experience for clues.

Another Way to Sell This Type of Book

Corporations can be potential subjects for books. Many corporate leaders are interested in having a book written about their company.

Here's a short plan to follow, if you'd like to try a company book:

1. Make a list from business directories found in the larger libraries. List the companies and corporations in your fields of interest and knowledge.

2. Write the public relations director or president of each company you select. Give some background information about yourself and describe any special knowledge or experience you have in connection with that company's business. Ask if there is any interest in a book related to the company.

3. Some companies may expect you to visit their offices to work out details on a book. Others can send you information you'll need in writing the book. If you know the business and have experience in it, a personal visit may not be needed.

4. A corporation may buy the book you write for them

outright, pay you royalties, or work out some other financial arrangement.

5. It might be advisable to choose companies located in your general area. Then, if they're interested in having you write books about their organizations, you can get to their offices for interviews and follow-up work on the book easily.

I believe this is an untapped market for possible new book sales for authors everywhere. You would naturally have to get the company brass interested in such a book project.

Some persuasion and sales ability would be in order. The truth is that any number of companies would really like to have books written about them, but they don't have the time for such a project. A number of managers of various business and professional associations have even admitted the need for books about their organizations. Some are actively looking for authors to write such books.

Most of the recognized book publishers in your country will send you copies of their latest catalogs at your request.

You can of course ask them in your letter if they publish business and professional books. If so, look over their titles in these areas after you receive their catalogs to get a good idea of their range of books in the business and professional markets.

Whether you try to place a book project with a recognized publisher or with a business corporation, you'll find some of the following directories and source books very helpful. They can usually be found in large libraries. Here are just a few:

National Directory of Associations
National Directory of Public Relations Directors
Gale's Encyclopedia of Associations
Public Relations Register
MacRae's Blue Book (Index of Companies)
Thomas Register of American Manufacturers

CHAPTER TWENTY-TWO

Textbooks Can Be a Money Jackpot

Some authors are not interested in writing textbooks. They're more interested in a standard nonfiction book or novel.

There are authors who cringe at the thought of doing a textbook. "All that technical and detailed work would get on my nerves," they say. "I'd rather write mass market paperbacks, children's books, or general nonfiction trade books."

No book about authorship is complete, however, without citing the case for writing one or more textbooks.

A successful textbook might well finance your writing work for some years to come.

Just one successful textbook used by the junior college market can bring in $20,000 a year or more for an author. This is assuming that the book sells for at least $11 to $13 a copy. Many such books sell at higher prices.

The beautiful thing about such textbooks is that they can keep bringing in handsome royalties for years. Some lucky authors with textbook sales call these books "golden annuities."

Textbooks are definitely worth the time and effort necessary to write and sell them. Or should I say sell and write them? Remember, the smart author sells first and then completes the manuscript.

With more and more quality and other paperbacks being used in the classroom today, textbooks don't have to be a mass of technical and complicated details. The accent now is on textbooks that communicate in a less technical way.

The trick to striking it rich with a textbook is to write one that is adopted by community colleges and/or regular four-year universities everywhere.

Textbooks that catch on can be used for many years. If they do become bibles in their respective subject areas, the authors are going to make a lot of money.

One highly acclaimed author wrote a math textbook a number of years back. He has reportedly realized well over a million dollars so far from this one book.

Royalties for Textbooks

Textbook royalties run from 8 to 12 percent (or higher) of the net price received by the publisher.

Schools and colleges order at bulk prices; authors' royalties are based on the net revenue received by a publisher for a specific textbook.

The author's royalties are considerably smaller for an elementary or high school textbook. Some authors with a good track record, however, may succeed in obtaining higher royalties.

You could possibly write a textbook for any of the following markets. Look them over to see what a potential bonanza your published text for these markets might be:

Elementary schools
High schools

Junior colleges
Community colleges
Four Year Universities
Graduate schools
Trade schools
Continuing Adult Education

If you've done any teaching, you may find it much easier to complete a textbook. The subject you taught would be a natural possibility.

I've taught journalism, creative writing, English, speech, literature, composition, and other courses on both the high school and college levels. I also once taught a course in religion.

As yet, I haven't tried my hand at writing a textbook on one of these subjects, but I will probably write one in the future.

Teaching experience is a definite advantage. After all, a teacher already knows a great deal about his chosen subject.

Another way to find a possible textbook subject is to search your memory. Think back on your school days. Which subjects did you enjoy the most? Write them down and decide on the one you like best. Then make a start.

Again, the best time to sell a textbook is before you're well into the book. Do an outline of what you would cover. Then try to interest a suitable textbook publisher.

You'll probably have to write one or more chapters at least, before trying to sell your book.

Chapter Thirty on markets in this book lists some likely publishers for a variety of textbooks.

The kind of money you can make from one or more textbooks is worth the investment of your time and effort. If one or more of your textbooks gets adopted by various schools, you'll be sitting pretty.

CHAPTER TWENTY-THREE

Mass Market Paperback Originals

Some of the biggest money an author can ever hope to make lies in mass market paperbacks. This might be the kind of writing for you.

Paul Little, a prolific author, first entered the paperback field in 1963. In just two years, he had twenty-six books published.

Paperbacks are published on a variety of subjects. Even the joys of reading have been written about in a paperback—*The New Hooked on Books*. This book has gone through more than ten editions.

Ballantine, the mass market paperback division of Random House, has a popular paperback out called *The Booze Battle*.

Author Cynthia Freeman started writing several years back, after giving up a career in interior design because of illness. Her very first novel, *A World Full of Strangers*, sold over two million copies in paperback. She found herself an overnight celebrity.

Fairytales, her second novel, relates the political rise and career of a young lawyer in San Francisco. Her book revolves around an Italian-American family.

The Test of a Mass Market Paperback Idea

Whenever you think you may have a hot idea for a mass market paperback, check it out with the following questions:

1. Would enough people be interested in the book? Mass market means appeal for millions of readers.
2. Do I have enough interest in the idea to see it through to completion? You'd be surprised how many manuscripts are started but never finished.
3. Is it commercial enough for the leading paperback publishers?

Getting the Feel for Mass Market Paperbacks

As you might expect, the best way to develop a feel for this kind of book is to read the novels of Harold Robbins, Jacqueline Susann, Rosemary Rogers, Peter Benchley, Mario Puzo, and other huge best sellers.

These authors, and others you can name yourself, have enormous appeal for the masses. Their books are filled with excitement, adventure, and glamour—all the ingredients that millions of readers cannot resist.

These books offer plenty of escape from the burdens, boredom, and disappointments of modern life.

The Beautiful Couple sold over a million paperback copies. Why? Read the book and note its great mass appeal.

Mass market paperbacks can be adventure novels, spy capers, historical novels, suspense thrillers, horror stories, or love stories. These books have plenty of action. They entertain the reader in a number of ways.

The Amazing Harold Robbins

Robbins is one of the best examples of a mass market author. He even calls himself the people's writer. His book sales prove it. Some of his previous books like *The Adventurers* and *The Carpetbaggers* sell a whopping ten million copies every year.

Robbins knows how to skillfully blend sin and sex into his novels. His characters are often beautiful people caught up in compelling situations. Now in his early 60s, Robbins continues to spin out his best-selling novels. One of his books, *The Pirate,* has just been produced as a television mini-series.

Robbins grew up in the Hell's Kitchen area of New York. But today he is a rich man, despite the fact that the government takes about 70 percent of his gross income.

When he's working on a book, he keeps the curtains drawn on the windows. He often uses a drab hotel room to do his writing. This method of isolation evidently works well for him.

One of his new books, *Memories of Another Day,* will no doubt chalk up huge sales figures. The book tells the story of the American labor movement and one ruthless man's rise to the top.

Mario Puzo: The Paperback Godfather

Time magazine has deemed best-selling author Mario Puzo the "paperback Godfather." The reprint rights for *Fools Die* were sold for an enormous amount of money. The book was on the best-seller lists long before its publication date.

The story takes place in Las Vegas and Puzo certainly writes with an understanding of the Vegas casinos. He's even written a book on gambling.

You don't have to read far in the book to notice Puzo's

outstanding descriptive abilities. He makes you see what's happening just like it's taking place on a stage before your eyes. The book runs 572 pages.

Robbins, Puzo, Susann, Irving Wallace, and other mass market authors obviously have the ability to take readers out of their daily routines. These authors lift such readers out of their humdrum lives and set them down in a variety of different worlds.

The Golden Future of Mass Market Paperbacks

Every sign indicates that this type of book is here to stay. With the population of the world increasing yearly and the four day work week already here in some places, there will be an even greater demand for books that entertain.

Who knows? You could be one of the celebrity authors of tomorrow, by developing the ability to give the mass reading public what it wants. Just one published book and you're on your way.

Whether you decide to specialize in this category one day or not, you should try in this area from time to time. You might just hit the paperback jackpot.

CHAPTER TWENTY-FOUR

Write That Self-Help Book

If nonfiction is the route you choose, perhaps completing an occasional novel, you should take careful aim at the self-help book.

Sales of self-help books are currently off a bit, but self-help is still one of the most profitable book categories available to any nonfiction author.

Millions of readers out there want help, all kinds of it. Life may have them uptight in one way or another. Or maybe they just haven't gotten the help they expected from magazines, newspapers, television, their doctors, lawyers, ministers, the government, or other sources.

The help they're seeking may be in a book on how to raise their children, how to guide them through the dangerous teen years, and how to pay the bill for their children's college education.

Maybe they want to lose weight, find a better doctor, plan a more exciting vacation, learn a new skill, develop a hobby, insulate their home, prevent a possible heart attack, or plan and give a speech.

There are a lot more potential subjects for a self-help book. The point of this type of book is that it offers practical help to the reader and gives specific information.

How to Know If You're Really in Love is a how-to title. But it's also a self-help book. Some titles bridge both categories.

The author of *How to Live With and Without Anger* has written about thirty-five self-help books. This is proof that some authors can find a profitable niche with this kind of book.

A glance at the shopping sections of leading mail-order publications shows that self-help books are selling by the carload.

The companies selling such books by mail wouldn't continue to run expensive ads for them if sales weren't brisk.

One sharp author sold the reprint rights to Bantam Books for his book, *How to Survive the Loss of a Love*. Rights were sold for a cool $165,000.

Why You Should Write a Self-Help Book

A case can be made for writing almost any kind of book. To help you decide if this is the right category for you, you might consider the following:

● You have a real interest in one or more self-help subjects.

● You have special knowledge, training, or experience in some area which can be applied to a self-help book.

● You enjoy helping others or would like to believe that a book you write might help at least a few people.

● You have access to the information needed for a book of this kind.

● The research needed for a book offering self-help seems interesting to you.

- You've developed a plan that has proven of some help to you. And you believe that others could profit from it too.
- Books in this category can stay in print for years.
- Many self-help books are financially profitable to their authors.

If none of the above seem to strike a chord within you, it doesn't mean that you can't write a self-help book. The items listed are meant to be a list of clues as to your potential as a self-help author.

How to Sell a Self-Help Book

Again, the process is similar to selling other kinds of books. In most cases, the following steps should help you to either get a contract from a publisher or at least some indication as to the merit of your book idea.

No author, however, should ever give up completely on a book project he or she still believes in. Authors have sold their books on the tenth, twenty-fifth, or sixtieth try. Here are the essential steps for selling a self-help book:

1. Pick a strong subject, preferably with a fresh angle on it, for a self-help book.

2. Write an outline or description of what you'd like to accomplish in the book. You may also wish to write a chapter or two.

3. Contact some publishers who are known to take this kind of book. Request a catalog and study their list of self-help titles. Some skip the catalog check, if they know the needs of various book publishers.

4. Describe your book project in a one- or two-page letter or send your outline or proposal to the appropriate editor.

You'll save time by writing a letter first. If the editor asks to see your project, you'll know there's some interest.

5. If rejected by one publisher, send it to another. Continue the process until your book is sold or you decide to

abandon the project. Don't give up hope on the book, even after ten or twenty publishers have turned it down. Keep trying other companies. Sometimes a slight bit of revision will get it placed.

CHAPTER TWENTY-FIVE

Overseas Publishers

If and when writing and selling books gets in your blood, you'll want to consider any worthy publisher for your various new projects. Depending upon the nature of each book, some publishers are naturally more suitable than others.

Regardless of where you now live, always remember that you're not limited to the book publishers in your country alone. Foreign publishers may be very interested in your new books.

There have been cases of authors in America, Canada, and other countries who couldn't find publishers for their books. Rather than give up, they offered their new book projects to publishers in Britain, Europe, Australia, Scotland, New Zealand, Germany, Spain, and other countries. And these publishers were pleased to get the new books.

So the point is not to overlook any recognized and respectable publisher worthy of the name.

There may be one or more overseas publishers and editors who would be delighted to accept your manuscript or book proposal, providing you have one ready to send.

At the end of this chapter, you'll find the names and current addresses of some book publishers in Canada, England, Japan, Australia, Europe, Spain, and the United States. Any one of the companies listed might possibly be interested in your book.

It's entirely possible that a published book of yours may chalk up only fair sales in your native country. On the other hand, that same book may take off and sell like mad in a foreign country.

Writing and Living in a Foreign Country

The careers of authors and entertainers alike have gotten real boosts, because these individuals moved to some other country.

Writing from overseas can give your entire work a fresh perspective. But there's more. An author living and working in London, Toronto, Paris, Tokyo, New York, Los Angeles, or some other center is bound to make new and valuable contacts in the book publishing business. One or more of these contacts could prove to be very helpful in the years ahead.

Janet Flanner's "Letter From Paris"

The late Janet Flanner, who wrote memorable columns for *The New Yorker* magazine for fifty years, was born in Indianapolis, Indiana and studied at the University of Chicago.

After working on Indiana newspapers, Janet toured Europe and settled in Paris in the early 1920s. Her "Letter from Paris" column and celebrity profiles established her as one of the finest writers of the century.

Selections from her column were put into a book called *Paris Journal, Volume I: 1944-65*. The volume won a National Book Award in the mid-1960s. Collections of the profiles she did were published as *An American in Paris* and *Paris Was Yesterday*.

There's certainly no guarantee that your writing will be more successful because you're living and working in a foreign country. But don't rule out the stimulation, contacts, and fresh viewpoint that can be gained from a stint abroad.

With the reduced air travel rates for people flying to and from America, Britain, Canada, Europe, and other countries, many people will have the opportunity to spend at least some time overseas.

Who knows what a month, six weeks, a summer, or a longer period of time might do for your writing.

Books by Overseas Publishers

Look at some of the following books published by overseas companies. Even this short list shows that the book business is alive, well, and enthusiastically producing some excellent books. Here are the titles:

Books by British Publishers

My Mother Said (a handbook of hints and old women's
    tales passed from generation to generation)
The Doyle Diary: The Last Great Conan Doyle Mystery
Love of London (a series book)
Your Hair: The Startling Facts
The Great Soccer Stars
Modern Cake Decoration
You Are Beautiful: And How to Prove It
The Cosmic Factor (ways the body is affected by the stars)

Books by Canadian Publishers (or Rights in Canada)

Guide to Canadian Business Law
The Great Canadian Explorer
A Divine Case of Murder
Your Baby Needs Music
Indigo Nights

Books by Japanese Publishers

Introducing Japan
Authority and the Individual in Japan: Citizen Protest in
*   Historical Perspective*
Teach Us to Outgrow Our Madness
The Sea and Poison
Best Karate (Eight Volume Series)

Books by Australian Publishers

The Hidden Powers of Leadership
Marriage and Personality
The Savage Crows
The History of the Car
Elvis Still Lives

Books by Spanish Publishers

The Great Spanish Cookbook
The Power of the Pyramids
The Black Monk
The Survivors of Atlantis

Books by Swedish Publishers

Carl Butler: Dine Well With Carl Butler
Death at the Circus
The Happy Year
Step by Step Cuisine

Coles Publishing Company (Canada)

One of the success stories in the publishing industry today is that of Coles Publishing Company. This enterprising Canadian company is not only actively engaged in publishing books on a variety of subjects; it also owns and operates a growing chain of over one hundred fifty bookstores in Canada and the United States.

Coles is dedicated to giving book buyers a lot of value for their money. Founded by Jack Cole, one of the chief lines of this publisher is self-help books.

They also do summary books on subjects like *Hamlet* and *Latin*. At this writing, Coles has several hundred book titles available.

An advantage for an author in placing one or more titles with Coles is the fact that the company has its own expanding chain of stores.

If Coles accepts one of your book projects, there is a strong possibility that the published book will be sold in all the stores of the Coles chain throughout Canada and the United States.

So you might keep this company in mind for the new books you write. Nonfiction books are what they want. Although the addresses of publishing companies change over a period of time, here is the current address of Coles:

Coles Publishing Company, Ltd.
90 Ronson Drive
Rexdale, Ontario, Canada M9W 1C1

The editorial director and vice-president of Coles Publishing Company is Jeffrey Cole. The company publishes both hardcover and paperback books. Some of their nonfiction interests include cooking, business, science, do-it-yourself topics, language, crafts and hobbies, the occult, reference, pet-care, and gardening.

Coles published about 300 books last year and will do 350 for this year. It's a growing company.

Australia

There are about 150 book publishers in Australia at this writing. Educational books accounted for 44 percent of the market last year. There are 14 million people in Australia. First hardcover printings range from 4,000 to 5,000 copies.

In general, books have a high mortality rate in Australia. A book doesn't stay on the best seller lists beyond a period of three months.

Paperback best sellers usually sell many more copies than hardcover books. *Dynasty* sold 8,000 in hardcover. But *The Exorcist* sold 175,000 in paperback.

The top selling paperback in the history of book sales in Australia (so far) was *Jaws*. It sold 750,000 copies. Many believe, however, that *The Thorn Birds* will do even better.

Great Britain

Last year, almost 40 percent of the sales of British book publishers came from exports. A recent study done on the way leisure time is spent in Britain revealed that only two hours a week are spent on reading out of a total of thirty-eight free hours.

Some of the publishers in Britain that continue to exert the greatest influence include Collins, Macmillan, Oxford University Press, Longman, Hodder and Stoughton, Cassell, Pan, Octopus, Pitman, and Hutchinson. Penguin currently leads the paperback market.

Collins alone published about 220 titles last year in Britain. About fifty books of this total were novels. Collins is easily the strongest British publisher on a world-wide basis.

Agents on the London book scene are busy and successful. There is strong interest in obtaining the British rights to commercial American books.

Book auctions are now a regular happening in London. The bids often run over $100,000. So you might give some thought to offering one of your book projects to British publishers at an auction. It helps to have an agent to do this, but some authors have managed nicely on their own.

A London Publisher You Might Try

If you decide to try to sell a book to a London publisher, you might consider contacting Hodder and Stoughton. This company publishes general trade books and also has a teach-yourself series, a religious list, an impressive children's line, and a paperback division known as Coronet.

In the words of Eric Major, who now runs the trade hardcover division, "It's the authors by whom a publishing house rises or falls. It's no good sitting back and declaring that a hardback publisher is merely in business these days for subsidiary rights: that's for agents. I believe we must go out and show we can and do sell books."

On the basis of this statement, it would seem that Hodder and Stoughton believes in putting a considerable amount of effort into promoting new authors.

So if you're a new author, or even an older pro, this might be the publisher for you, no matter what country you call home.

See the additional market listings in Chapter Thirty for more possible publishers for your books. I say books, because I hope you'll be writing many of them in the future.

CHAPTER TWENTY-SIX

Book Publishers Are Waiting with Contracts

I hope by this point that you see the great potential for authors in today's world of books.

I want you to be enthusiastic over your chances to place one or more of your books. Publishers are waiting with fair, or even juicy, contracts. Authors are in demand.

All you need is a partial manuscript or outline and a few chapters. Even just an idea for a book may be enough to lead you to an eventual book sale.

How to Make More Book Sales

Get to know the needs of publishers. There are too many authors who send material to publishers without making any effort to learn their needs.

Maybe a certain company doesn't want any more cookbooks, or how-tos, or Gothic novels. You'll save time and postage by first sounding out a publisher on current needs and interests. For example, I contacted a New York hard-cover publisher several months back. While the book projects I sent to them came close, they were not accepted. But a top executive of this company advised me to get in touch with him a bit later. The company was planning to start a new paperback division, and some of the projects I had submitted looked right.

The point is that many authors don't know what the current situation is at a given publishing office, unless they have an inside contact. So instead of sending in a manu-script or proposal cold, it's far better, nine times out of ten, to send a letter first. Ask what their current needs are for new books or if a certain book category is within their scope.

Make it a regular practice to study the market listings of book publishers. They can be found in the annual editions of *Literary Market Place* and *Writer's Market*. These list-ings tell you what categories the publishers want and also give some titles of books recently published.

Some authors are able to see editors in person to check on their current subject interests. Authors who live in New York, London, Chicago, Toronto, Sydney, Los Angeles, Paris, and other centers have a better chance to meet with editors or talk to them on the phone in order to discover their new book needs. At the same time, many editors prefer letters from authors instead of personal visits. It saves their time. And the editor can study the written description or query letter regarding a new book idea at his or her convenience.

The following is a list of things to keep in mind when contacting a publisher:

● Don't send a book on pet-care to a publisher of busi-ness books. Find out first through market listings or a letter if the publisher's interests match up with your par-ticular book project.

Believe it or not, there are authors who send in their

completed novels to publishers who accept only nonfiction books.

If you intend to write books, some of your time must be spent on deciding who the right publishers are for each of your books.

Make a list of the most likely publishers and then try each one until you make a sale or decide to temporarily scrap the project.

• Good timing can mean a sale. Sometimes a publisher will want a book project, in order to keep the office staff busy or to reach a goal of so many new books contracted for in a year's time. There are various reasons for acceptance.

Maybe a certain publisher wants three more historical romances before Christmas, an occult title, a work of history to tie in with an upcoming observance, a travel book for the next year's summer vacation season, or a career book for young people.

The point is that good timing alone can bring you extra book sales. When your material arrives can have a real influence on whether or not a sale is made.

Try Small, Medium, and Large Publishers

You can sell a book to a small or medium publisher, if one of the giant companies turns it down. Never believe that you're licked, just because a big publisher says no. You still have other large companies to try, along with medium and smaller publishers.

Try Many Publishers

There are thousands of book publishers today in a number of countries. Make up your mind now to try at least ten, twenty-five, fifty, or more before you even think about giving up on that particular book project.

In between submissions, you can of course be polishing up your project. You may rewrite it one or more times. The point I wish to make is that a real author never gives up on a book he or she believes in and knows should be published.

Let no publisher or group of them ever discourage you. Some of the greatest success stories became realities because authors or creators refused to quit trying.

Key Sources for Markets

Writer's Market (published yearly)
9933 Alliance Road
Cincinnati, Ohio 45242

Literary Market Place (published yearly)
R. R. Bowker
1180 Avenue of the Americas
New York, New York 10036

CHAPTER TWENTY-SEVEN

Get Thee to the ABA Convention

There are authors, both established professionals and beginners, who occasionally comment on the fact that most working authors spend much of their time alone. The solitary nature of the craft calls for it.

Whether you write a novel or a nonfiction book, the process of putting words down on paper means spending long hours alone. So the annual ABA convention is a godsend for an author.

What is the ABA convention? The letters ABA stand for the American Booksellers Association. Thousands of key people who own and operate bookstores across the country attend this important convention each year. It's one of the major events of the book publishing industry. The ABA convention is a yearly opportunity for booksellers, publishers, sales representatives, distributors, and authors to meet together for several days.

The key purpose of the convention is to aid booksellers

in their business of ordering and merchandising all kinds of books. The booksellers are the stars and the main reason for the convention. Everything planned and presented on the ABA program is meant to help all booksellers run a smoother and more profitable business.

Foreign publishers are well represented at the convention. Just about every country that sells books had key people from the publishing industry on the scene for last year's convention held in Atlanta. No matter what kind of author you are, your presence at the ABA convention is a must.

The ABA Convention Is Fabulous

If you love books, and most authors do, you simply can't miss the ABA convention. I would personally rate an author's attendance at the annual ABA meeting as a four-star must for the following reasons:

• Most consider it the most important single event in the entire book business for the year.

• You have a chance to talk to many of the key booksellers in the country. You thus get their views on new trends in publishing, various industry problems, and reactions to various books.

After all, these are the people who sell the books written by authors. They're important industry people to know and can help you attain your goals as an author.

• By visiting the booths on the convention floor, you see in advance the books soon to be published. You also see the current best-selling titles and old standbys.

These benefits are well worth the time and expense of attending the convention. I have yet to meet an author who isn't enthusiastic and stimulated by seeing all the new and recent books on display at the ABA.

• An author who attends ABA conventions develops a much better understanding of each·publisher's line of books. You won't remember them all; there are too many publishers represented. But you do gain a better grasp of the style of many leading book publishers.

● You obviously meet a number of bookstore owners, editors from publishing companies, sales representatives, and possibly agents. The point is that you're bound to make some good contacts.

● The ABA presents excellent seminars on various industry topics. You're welcome to sit in on them and take part in the question-answer sessions, which are usually held at the end of the seminars.

● All new catalogs of publishers plus advertising materials on new books are available at each booth. You're welcome to them as you pass each booth on the convention floor. Special issues of the leading book trade publications such as *American Bookseller* magazine and *Publishers Weekly* are also free.

● You get to attend several banquets and numerous cocktail parties. There's a reasonable charge for the banquets.

● The ABA special breakfast programs are quite popular. They start early in the morning but are well attended. Well-known authors usually speak at these breakfast programs.

● Music, the chance to hear relevant topics discussed, the opportunity to renew old friendships with colleagues in the business, and food and drink are some of the attractions at the conventions.

● The convention usually lasts four or five days. The length may be extended in future years. It's a great way to spend some time away from your writing desk. You'll go back to your writing relaxed, enthusiastic, and filled with renewed vigor.

● The ABA convention is inspiring in a number of ways for an author. You just come away with a better appreciation and feeling for book publishing as a whole and your part in it.

How Last Year's ABA Convention Helped Me as an Author

I find each ABA convention a fabulous event. When one convention ends, I start looking forward to the next. Here are just a few of the pluses I got from last year's meeting:

1. I made some wonderful new contacts among publishers, booksellers, authors, and other industry people.

2. I personally talked to a dozen top editors at leading publishing companies.

3. I met and chatted with other editorial and sales people from about thirty book publishers.

4. While I did not plug or attempt to sell any of my new book projects (Authors are requested not to do this during the convention.), five editors asked to see my new book projects when ready. They suggested that I send some material to them.

5. I personally met a number of celebrity authors including Lauren Bacall, Anne Baxter, Mel Torme, and Dale Evans Rogers.

6. I met and talked with fifty or more booksellers and bookstore managers from all parts of the country. Many of them praised and commented on my book *How to Write Songs That Sell*, which has become a backlist title.

Some bookstore operators in the Midwest said that they couldn't keep my book in stock, because it sells out every time. One bookseller remarked that buyers of my songwriting book had claimed that it was more helpful than other such books.

This is the sort of experience that gives an author a real boost. Authors work hard on their books. Any words of praise are most welcome and satisfying.

7. I feasted on the overwhelming display of new novels and nonfiction books on all kinds of subjects.

8. I gained a much clearer idea of the bookseller's role in selling books. The job involves far more paperwork than I had realized. Booksellers have lots of problems, but

most of them remain enthusiastic about selling books.

9. I came away greatly inspired despite my tired and sore feet (from walking the convention floor for four days). I'm more proud than ever to be a part of the fascinating book business. Getting back to my writing was easy, after four marvelous days at the ABA.

10. I came home with a dozen new book and article ideas. I sold several of these a few months later.

ABA Breakfast Program Highlights

Mel Torme—Speaking about how he got started as a singer and entertainer. His comments about his novel, *Wynner*, were most interesting: "I hope you'll think of me as a writer who occasionally sings."

Other remarks by Mel: "People I meet on planes ask me if I really wrote *Wynner* myself." He did indeed.

Ruth Carter Stapleton—About her book on Billy Carter: "Billy knows how to live for the moment and how not to worry."

Ray Charles—Speaking about his early career, the subject of his new book, *Brother Ray:* "I don't know what kind of music I'm into. I like to think of myself as a good utility man." Ray made it clear that he wanted his book to sound like him.

Questions Asked by Booksellers

A final program on the last day of the convention featured the key questions of booksellers. The questions were directed to a distinguished fourteen-member panel of leading book publishers. Some of the subjects discussed were the length of time it takes to receive credits, insurance for book shipments, communication problems between booksellers and publishers, the discrepancy in the length of time it takes to receive orders of varying sizes, the service role of sales representatives, rising postage rates, and customer service matters.

How and When You Can Attend the ABA Convention

The basic requirement for an author to attend the ABA convention is having published at least one book.

If you have some legitimate connection with the book industry, however, you would be welcome at the ABA. The men and women who work in bookstores across the country are of course in attendance. Many bookstores send at least a few delegates each year, depending on their size.

Most of the convention programs call for tickets. If and when you plan to attend one of the conventions, I advise you to write the ABA office in New York well in advance of the meeting. Ask that full information be sent to you about the convention when it's available.

The tickets to the convention may be obtained in advance. When you know the city location of each new convention, line up your hotel reservations early. The crowd attending the ABA seems to grow larger every year. So make your plans early. Get your name listed early and order your program tickets far in advance. You'll be glad you did. For details write:

American Booksellers Association, Inc.
122 East 42nd Street
New York, New York 10017

CHAPTER TWENTY-EIGHT

Promotional Opportunities for Your Book

In this chapter I'll be discussing the promotion of your books. As mentioned earlier, some authors forget a book once it's been published. They're usually involved in a new project by then.

There are two types of promotion—what your publisher can do for the book and what you can accomplish yourself. Anything you can do for each of your books will help, so keep this fact in mind.

There are positive things you can do to promote your book. If you can't drive across the country seeing bookstore managers about your book, you can take other steps.

To refresh your memory and give you a workable promotion plan, refer back to this chapter each time one of your books is published. Here is the plan:

1. Make the rounds of all the book stores in your area. Tell them about your book and try to arrange an autograph session in some of the major stores. Many bookstore

operators are receptive to having authors appear in their stores. Such appearances sell books.

2. Do anything you can to get on local radio and television programs. You can write the station or specific talk show personality, or go to the station in person. You'll probably have to make an appointment to see the program manager, public relations director, or appropriate person.

3. Tell everyone about your book and write letters about it to all your friends and relatives.

4. Try to interest local newspaper writers in doing a feature about you and your book. Most city papers have a book review or literary section. Call or write the newspaper and ask who you should contact. Try to get a personal meeting with the right editor or writer.

5. Contact any and all trade journals and publications about your book. If your book is on pet-care, for example, the leading magazines in the pet industry could be contacted. If your book covers a business subject, there are numerous publications you can contact.

6. Consider the idea of writing a feature article about your book yourself. It's possible that a national, regional, or local magazine or newspaper might use it.

I've done this myself a number of times. If your book is timely, chances are even better that your article will be used.

7. Watch the book trade publications like *Publishers Weekly* for leads on book reviewers. The circulations of these newspapers and magazines are large.

8. Quite a few daily newspapers have a Sunday magazine section. Write to the managing editor of each about your book. Included in the list are the *Chicago Tribune Magazine, Family Weekly, The New York Times Magazine, Parade, Columbus Dispatch Sunday Magazine, Seattle Times Magazine,* and *Weekend Magazine* (in Toronto, Canada).

9. Look for some angle that a magazine or newspaper

editor could use to publicize your book. For example, will it help readers save money, learn the truth about something, make more money, or move up on the job?

The Following People Could Be Helpful in Promoting Your Book

Booksellers
Librarians
Advertising people
Book reviewers
Book salespeople
Columnists
Fraternal club officers
Civic club leaders
Radio and television personalities
Editors of magazines, newspapers, trade journals, newsletters, and bulletins and fraternity-sorority magazines
Public relations directors
Club women
Historical societies
All kinds of special clubs and hobby groups
National and international association directors
Book club officials
Fraternities and sororities

10. Write out an effective direct sales letter in which you tell about your book and yourself. Send the letter to a list of radio and television stations that might be receptive to having you as a guest author.

You can also send the same letter to anyone you think might help promote your book.

11. Consider "self-syndicating" a feature article or review about your book. You can get the names of a great many newspaper editors in yearly syndicate directories published by *Editor and Publisher*.

12. Work up an oral presentation in which you talk about your book; for example, discuss why you wrote it. Prepare a professional-looking pamphlet highlighting the features of your talk and telling something about your background. Have a number of copies printed then send them to anyone and everyone who might book you on a program as a speaker. A number of authors do very nicely working side dates as speakers in between their writing projects or while they're writing.

Publicity Stunts

If you're an imaginative and somewhat daring type of author, you might also consider dreaming up some kind of publicity stunt to attract attention to your book.

A man who ran for governor of Tennessee walked across the entire state. He received regular and continuous publicity for the walk and was shown talking to people all along the way.

He made a mark at the end of each day, to show where he had stopped. He then resumed his walk at his marker the next day. It was an effective idea and worked well for him.

There may be one or more clues in your book for a possible publicity stunt. The questions to ask include the following:

1. What could I do to attract favorable publicity for my book?

2. Are there any unusual ways to advertise and promote my book?

3. Could I arrange to get any local, regional, or national celebrity to plug my book?

4. Is there anything unique, shocking, timely, or newsworthy about my book that might get me an interview on the "Today," "Tonight," or "Tomorrow" television shows? "The Phil Donahue Show" and "Good Morning,

America" are also excellent programs for authors. Find
out who interviews authors for possible bookings on these
shows. You might just land on one.

5. Could I do something dramatic that might increase
the sales of my book like bicycle across the nation or rent a
billboard sign?

Get in Touch with Newspaper Columnists

There are columns written on all kinds of subjects. Your
book might be interesting to the readers of columns on
life-styles, business, money matters, self-help topics, cooking, marriage, or whatever. The circulation of many columns runs in the hundreds of thousands or even the
millions. A mention of your book by the columnist could
be a real promotional shot in the arm for your book.

Here are some national columnists and their addresses.
The titles of their columns are also listed. Please realize
that the addresses given are current at this writing. Here
they are:

Book Columnists

Ralph Hollenbeck ("Parade of Books")
King Features Syndicate
235 East 45th Street
New York, New York 10017

William McPherson ("Book World")
Washington Post
1150 15th Street, N.W.
Washington, D.C. 20071

Robert Kirsch ("The Book Report")
11045 Camarillo Street
North Hollywood, California 90602

Carol Felsenthal ("About Books")
American Library Association
50 E. Huron Street
Chicago, Illinois 60611

Here are some book reviewers who might consider your book. Any publicity can be helpful. Again, the addresses may be subject to change. Here they are:

"The Lewis Meyer Book Shelf"
KOTV in Tulsa, Oklahoma
Lewis Meyer
1308 E. 19th Street
Tulsa, Oklahoma 74120

Los Angeles Times
Book Review Section
Art Seidenbaum (current editor)
Times Mirror Square
Los Angeles, California 90053

Sunday Book Review Section
Ed Hutsching (Book editor)
Dorothy Allshouse ("Paperback Parade")
San Diego Union
350 Camino de la Reina
San Diego, California 92112

Nancy Evans (Reviewer)
Glamour Magazine
350 Madison Avenue
New York, New York 10017

Charles Trueheart, Book Editor
The News-American
Lombard & South Streets
Baltimore, Maryland 21203

Michael J. Bandler, Book Editor
(Book column for *American Way,* the monthly magazine
    of American Airlines)
1101 N. Belgrade Road
Silver Spring, Maryland 20902
(Column has a lead time of ten weeks)

Other Important Promotional Addresses

"A Word on Words" (television show that features authors
    and books)
John Seigenthaler (host and publisher of *The Tennessean
    Newspaper*)
Contact Mike Kroger, Producer
WDCN-TV
161 Rains Avenue
Nashville, Tennessee 37203

Column called "Book Marker"
Bestways-The Magazine for a Better way to Health (health-
    cookbooks)
Rustie Brown (reviewer)
1650 W. 247th Place
Harbor City, California 90710

Weekly book review column—"Have You Read?"
(combines author interviews with reviews)
Contact: Joan Swain
4 Olcott Lane
Bernardsville, New Jersey 07924

CHAPTER TWENTY-NINE

The Truth about Self-Publishing

If you cannot find a worthy publisher to handle your book, another avenue is open to you before scrapping the project. You can publish your book yourself.

I don't advise you to go this route, unless most or all of the following factors are true in your case:

1. You've tried thirty or more recognized book publishers, and all of them have rejected your project. Many authors try fifty or more companies before giving up. Some never give up.

2. You're hell-bent on seeing your book published, no matter what.

3. You have the money necessary to finance the publication of your own book, along with some promotion for it.

4. You have a strong belief that your book will sell.

5. You have a nagging feeling that you should publish the book.

The truth about self-publishing is that it can go either

way for an author. Some authors have lost most or all of their money on self-published projects. Others have regained their investments and a small profit. Still others have done amazingly well with their self-published books. Some of the luckier wordsmiths have realized large cash jackpots, usually after considerable effort, promotion, and even personal selling campaigns.

The Concept of Self-Publishing

The self-publishing view is that just about anybody with a good book idea can publish his or her own manuscript, provided there is money available.

Here are a few examples of self-published books: *Marling Menu-Masters*—Menu guides that sold at $2.95 in Spain, Germany, and Italy. Over 100,000 sold in Europe to American families stationed overseas. They're now also selling well in the United States.

City Survival Suite—A book of poems published by a southern poet at a cost of $240 for 200 copies. The author's main objectives are to get the book out and get his name recognized.

All manner of mail-order books and booklets are sold on a wide variety of subjects from how to stop smoking to building a more successful career. Books on solar energy are currently selling well by mail. The owner-publisher of such books runs classified ads in leading mail-order publications, filling orders as they're received. Some do quite well via mail-order.

A few years ago, a successful woman lawyer in the Midwest finished a first novel and sent it off to a likely publisher. After six months of waiting, her manuscript was finally returned. Undaunted, she sent it off to another publisher. After a year-and-a-half passed, she finally received another rejection. So what did she do? She published it herself, doing the artwork and handling the printing and distribution of the book.

Her book started selling and soon attracted a West Coast agent, who signed the self-published author-lawyer as a client. Her agent sold the paperback rights for a large sum.

Success Can Come Via the Do-It-Yourself Method

So the point is that success can come through the do-it-yourself method. It's a start, a way to hang in there and maybe beat all the odds against you.

One first novelist in California has made money by selling his self-published novel door to door. He has every right to call himself a published author.

So there's just no telling where a self-publishing venture might lead you. Do your best to find a recognized publisher for your book. But always think about self-publishing, if and when you cannot place your book.

A number of successful writing careers have been launched by self-publishing. It might work for you. And once your self-published book proves itself in the market, you'll find little trouble placing your next book. An author is only as good as his or her latest book, but a track record can open doors that were previously closed to you.

CHAPTER THIRTY

Markets for Your Book

The following list of markets is not a complete one. It's meant to be a quick reference for at least several possible markets for your new books. Large and powerful publishers are included, along with medium-sized and smaller ones.

The list also covers some newer companies and addresses of a number of agents who might consider representing you. Be sure to write them first for permission to send any material.

Again, keep in mind that all of the following addresses are subject to change. When in doubt about an address of a publisher, I suggest that you check the yearly editions of *Literary Market Place* or *Writer's Market*. Here is the market list:

Mass Market Paperback Originals

Bantam Books, Inc.
666 Fifth Avenue
New York, New York 10019

Avon Books
959 Eighth Avenue
New York, New York 10019

Berkley Publishing Corporation
200 Madison Avenue
New York, New York 10016

Fawcett Crest and Gold Medal Books
1515 Broadway
New York, New York 10036

Ballantine Books
201 East 50th Street
New York, New York 10022

Pocket Books
1230 Avenue of the Americas
New York, New York 10020

Penguin Books
625 Madison Avenue
New York, New York 10022

General Nonfiction (most categories)

G. P. Putnam's Sons
200 Madison Avenue
New York, New York 10016

Little, Brown and Company (some how-to)
34 Beacon Street
Boston, Massachusetts 02106

Simon and Schuster (Trade Division)
1230 Sixth Avenue
New York, New York 10020

Rand McNally
P.O. Box 7600
Chicago, Illinois 60680

Prentice-Hall, Inc.
Englewood Cliffs, New Jersey 07632

Grosset and Dunlap
51 Madison Avenue
New York, New York 10010

General Fiction (Novels)

Contemporary Books
180 North Michigan Avenue
Chicago, Illinois 60601

Crown Publishers
1 Park Avenue
New York, New York 10016

Macmillan Publishing Company
866 Third Avenue
New York, New York 10022

Dodd, Mead & Company
79 Madison Avenue
New York, New York 10016

E. P. Dutton
201 Park Avenue South
New York, New York 10003

Major Books
21335 Roscoe Boulevard
Canoga Park, California 91304

Religious-Inspirational

Fleming H. Revell Company
Central Avenue
Old Tappan, New Jersey 07675

Baker Book House Company
Box 6287
Grand Rapids, Michigan 49506

Tyndale House Publishers
336 Gundersen Drive
Wheaton, Illinois 60187

Herald Press
616 Walnut Avenue
Scottdale, Pennsylvania 15683

Thomas Nelson, Inc.
30 East 42nd Street
New York, New York 10017

Chosen Books
Lincoln, Virginia 22078

Business-Professional

RD Communications
Box 683
Ridgefield, Connecticut 06877

Wilshire Book Company (business)
12015 Sherman Road
North Hollywood, California 91605

Parker Publishing Company
West Nyack, New York 10994

B. Klein Publications
Box 8503
Coral Springs, Florida 33065

Textbooks

McGraw-Hill Book Company
1221 Avenue of the Americas
New York, New York 10020

New Viewpoints
Division of Franklin Watts
730 Fifth Avenue
New York, New York 10019

National Textbook Company
8259 Niles Center Road
Skokie, Illinois 60076

Rand McNally
P.O. Box 7600
Chicago, Illinois 60680

Juvenile Publishers

Prentice-Hall
Englewood Cliffs, New Jersey 07632

The Viking Press
625 Madison Avenue
New York, New York 10022

Random House, Inc.
201 East 50th Street
New York, New York 10022

Franklin Watts, Inc.
730 Fifth Avenue
New York, New York 10019

Miscellaneous

Contemporary Books
180 North Michigan Avenue
Chicago, Illinois 60601

Grosset and Dunlap
51 Madison Avenue
New York, New York 10010

Chilton Book Company
201 King of Prussia Road
Radnor, Pennsylvania 19089

Follett Publishing Company
1010 W. Washington
Chicago, Illinois 60607

Historical Romances

See the companies listed under Mass Market Paperback
Originals.

Literary Agents

Julian Bach Agency
3 East 48th Street
New York, New York 10017

Donald MacCampbell, Inc.
12 East 41st Street
New York, New York 10017
(Book-length fiction only)

James Brown Associates, Inc.
25 West 43rd Street
New York, New York 10036

Arthur Pine Associates, Inc.
1780 Broadway
New York, New York 10019

The Richard Curtis Literary Agency
156 East 52nd Street
New York, New York 10022

Collier Associates
280 Madison Avenue
New York, New York 10016

Charles R. Byrne Agency
1133 Avenue of Americas
28th Floor
New York, New York 10036

Julie Ann Gordon
150 East 56th Street
New York, New York 10022

No editorial names are given for the above list of book publishers. The reason is that there are frequent changes in publishing houses. Assistant and associate editors become senior editors. Editors-in-chief move to other companies. Such changes go on continually. Check *Literary Market Place* for the names of editors. You will also find key editorial names in each issue of *Publishers Weekly*.

Important Publications You Should Read

Publishers Weekly (I recommend that you subscribe to it.)
1180 Avenue of the Americas
New York, New York 10036.

Quill and Quire (Covers the book trade in Canada)
59 Front Street, East
Toronto, Ontario, Canada M5E 1B3

The Bookseller (Organ of the book trade in England)
12 Dyott Street
London WC1A 1DF, England

Christian Bookseller Magazine
Gundersen and Schmale Road
Wheaton, Illinois 60187
(Good overall view of religious-inspirational book field)

CHAPTER THIRTY-ONE

Some Four-Star Parting Advice

I believe the following advice will prove to be helpful to you as you write and sell your new books. This advice is based on my experience in the book business. It should save you time, effort, and discouragement. Here it is:

Once you find a publisher who treats you fairly and professionally, stick with that company.

Think in terms of what will interest and help readers.

Every time you mail out a manuscript or proposal, realize that you're gambling. Your material may not get there. It may be lost, stolen, or come back to you in shredded condition. This happens to about 5 percent of the material you send out. Just know that with today's mail service (especially in the United States), each of your submissions is a gamble in several ways.

If you hope to eventually write for a living you should try every field you can which might be financially promising.

"The impossible is just something nobody has done yet."

The query letter gives you psychological insurance. Do not send in material cold to a publisher. Always write a letter first.

Remember that as an author, you can go anywhere. All you need are pencils, pens, paper, and a typewriter. Authors are some of the freest people in the world.

Many books are considered successes, though they may sell far less than a best seller.

It's easier to write a book on one subject than to research twenty or thirty different subjects for nonfiction articles.

Book publishers are in the business of selling ideas.

You should have at least one or more self-help books in you. *How to Win Over Worry* sold 330,000 copies (to date) for Zondervan.

If you live outside the New York area, it's usually better to have an agent.

The staple of most book publishers is the trade book.

Send out many ideas for new book projects. You just can't tell what might strike an editor's fancy.

Try to write as if you think writing is fun. It is for many

authors. Make your readers enjoy what you say between page one and the final page.

Many books seek only to entertain the reader and often become best sellers because they do it so well.

In most cases, an outline will make it easier to write your book.

Stay interested in many facets of life. The ideas will then be more likely to come.

The first book an author does is often the hardest. It gets a lot easier after the first time at bat.

"Clear writing is clear thinking." Many a good book has been written on this basic premise.

Germany is a big book market. The West Germans are big readers.

One good way to stay enthusiastic as an author is to read *Publishers Weekly* from cover to cover. It's the bible of the book world.

It helps to check *Books in Print* to see what other books have been published on a particular subject.

Enough research lets you know if an idea is really a good one.

Some book outlines don't take too much time. Others require a lot of thought and work. But they can pay off handsomely.

Playing the game of "what if" is a useful beginning for a novel.

Laurence Sterne didn't realize how talented he was as an author until about nine years before his death.

One author traveled some 16,000 miles all over the country to visit amusement parks. She was gathering material for a book on merry-go-rounds.

Mark Twain convinced Ulysses Grant to write his memoirs for 70 percent of the net profits. The heirs of Grant realized more than $420,000 in royalties from the two volumes. That was quite a fortune in 1885.

Sherwood Anderson said, "Words are the greatest things ever invented."

Deadlines in a book contract help an author to finish a project. Most book contracts state when a manuscript is to be delivered.

What makes a book sell is usually word-of-mouth recommendation. But anything an author can do for his or her book will help.

An increasing number of publishers tend to go for the big commercial book. They back such books with more money, promotion, and advertising. Some books still sell, even if a firm does nothing.

Try your hand occasionally at a paperback original.

One book club paid five figures for a title on knitting. Try to pick timeless subjects that will be continuous sellers.

Books are noble things. They can bring you fame and fortune.

Index